P9-DCO-286

8016

970.4 Keithahn, Edward L.
K   Monuments in cedar.

8016

970.4   Keithahn, Edward Linnaeus
K   Monuments in cedar.   Superior, 1963.

1. Indians of North America - Northwest,
Pacific 2. Totems and totemism I. T.

MONUMENTS IN CEDAR

Monument, mystical, awesome and ghoulish;
Seemingly purposeless, paganish, foolish;
What is the message your symbols conceal?
Strong the incentive of him that conceived thee
Leaving to adept, its truth to reveal.

From "The Totem Pole"
by Dr. E. Van Note

MONUMENTS IN CEDAR

BY

EDWARD L. KEITHAHN

Superior PUBLISHING COMPANY

SEATTLE, WASHINGTON
1963

Dedication

This volume is dedicated to the memory of those early Alaskan and Northwest Coast photographers, amateur as well as professional, whose pictures have not only made illustration of the text possible, but have helped immeasureably in preserving a memory of some of the world's most interesting sculptured monuments which, being of wood are highly perishable. In consequence, most have been lost except in memory or replica and only by photographs do we know of them.

Among those whose memory I wish to honor are Juneau and Skagway photographer, W. H. Case of the firm of Case & Draper; Lloyd Winter and Percy Pond of the firm of Winter & Pond and the Harrison Brothers. Pioneer Sitka photographers were Reuben Albertstone, Edward de Groff and E. W. Merrill; Wrangell is represented by J. E. Worden and Dr. Fred W. Carlyon; Douglas by Ed Andrews, Angoon by Vincent Soboleff, Klukwan by Louis Shotridge and Yakutat by Fhoki Kayamori.

From the states came other early photographers, mostly single-trippers who were attracted by the weird sculptures of the native marine Indians and recorded them on the glass plates of the day. Among these were Edward L. Curtis and F. La Roche of Seattle, E. W. Partridge and Davidson of Portland; Miles Brothers of San Francisco and Merle La Voy. No doubt many others recorded the native villages and their totem clusters but so far their plates, if they still exist, have not come to the attention of the author.

Preface

In the first edition of *Monuments in Cedar,* published in 1945, I mentioned that I had seen my first totem poles at the Alaska Yukon Pacific Exposition in Seattle in 1909. Whether it was actually on the fair grounds or in Pioneer Square I no longer remember, but I was impressed. Fourteen years later, on my first trip into the land where totem poles come from, I saw clusters of them, *in situ,* at Bella Bella, Alert Bay, and at Ketchikan. This whetted my early curiosity as to what they really stood for. But, upon inquiry at that time, nobody seemed to know or even care.

It is now 35 years since we came to the land of totem poles to live. From the Indian Service for whom I eventually taught totem carving and native culture at Wrangell Institute, I went in 1941 to the Alaska Historical Library and Museum at Juneau to be Curator and Librarian for the then Territory of Alaska. There, surrounded by a growing collection of the art and artifacts of these aboriginal rain foresters and the collected writings about them, I could at last converse via the printed page with 18th and 19th century informants who spoke European languages.

In the meanwhile nearly all of my original native informants have passed on and I sincerely miss them. There are still questions I forgot to ask; points I would like to clear up. Perhaps they couldn't have helped, anyway, for as one informant recently put it, 'We didn't know enough English in those days to tell you what we knew." Another, when asked upon his return to his village to question the oldtimers exclaimed, "Keithahn, *you* and *I* are the *oldtimers!"*

Lately, great changes have been taking place in the land of the totem pole. Alaska has become a state; the dripping rain forests now support huge pulp and lumber mills; the fisheries, once almost lost, are being restored and expanded. A marine highway links the island ports with each other and with the mainland accesses to the interior. Tuberculosis in its many malignant forms, once the curse of the native peoples, is under control and the Indian population is burgeoning. Indian leaders sit in both houses of the State Legislature; young Indians of both sexes hold responsible positions in both state and federal offices.

Still more gratifying is the knowledge that native arts and crafts have lately experienced a new appreciation as ways to adapt Northwest Coast sculpture and decorative art to modern usage have been discovered. Native dances have been revived and this has occassioned the manufacture of dancing costumes and accessories such as headdresses, robes, batons, masks, drums and rattles. Decorative panels and sculptures are appearing in homes and public places. The decor of the new Alaska ferry liners is in Northwest Coast Indian style. And with a new demand for full scale totem poles and other sculptures, the professional Indian carver has again appeared on the scene, demonstrating again the immortality of a great art style and tradition and its ability to survive in rapidly changing times.

I shall not repeat the names of all those informants who contributed to the success of the first edition for nearly all of them are gone. But they were many: Tlingit, Haida, Tsimshian, pioneers. Now the list has grown to include a great host who live or had lived somewhere between Ketchikan and Katalla or on the British Columbian coast. Each of these contributed a fact or a thought or an artifact or a photograph that helped to tell the story of totem poles, the allied arts and crafts, and the peoples responsible for them. To all of these unnamed friends, I am sincerely grateful and give my thanks.

THE HAIDA VILLAGE OF SKIDEGATE, QUEEN CHARLOTTE ISLANDS.

This photograph, taken in 1878 by Dr. George M. Dawson, is a classic view of a Northwest Coast village near the close of the Golden Age. Without such a photograph one would surely be misled by a traveler's report that such villages were fronted by a "thicket of totem sticks." A Hudson's Bay "point" blanket is draped across a canoe to prevent checking. Four people may be seen sitting on a platform above the XX.

Photo Credit: Provincial Archives
Victoria, B.C.

Below: **BELLA COOLA HOUSE FRONTAL POLE** Thunderbird Park, Victoria.

CONTENTS

THE COLOR PHOTOGRAPHS

SUN AND RAVEN POLE. This *Sun and Raven* pole is a restoration of one from a cemetery on Pennock Island which was intended to be a copy of an earlier one standing in Tongass Village. But the new pole was short, so the carving was compressed somewhat, only the face of the fog woman remaining of the complete figure in the original pole. Here we see three of *Raven's* adventures: his escape from the flood during which time he was guest of *Sun* and played with *Sun's* three children shown here. The Sun halo around Raven's head is intended to recall this incident. Raven's affair with *Fog Woman* recalled in the center of the pole is best told on Chief Johnson's pole (see text).

Once when *Raven* expressed a wish to explore the bottom of the sea, *Frog* volunteered to accompany him as a servant. The two are shown together in the lower panel.

Jacket and Page 2

KATSEEK SCREEN. Generally speaking, the Chilkat Tlingit have considered their crests too sacred to be viewed by the general public except on auspicious occasions. But Katseek, late *Tlingit-klen* (big man) or Head Chief of the Duklawadi Clan thought otherwise. He held open house to all visitors (tourists included) until his death in 1961. The heraldic screen of the Killerwhale Fin House shown here consists of eight carved and painted panels, displaying clan symbols of the Duklawadi Clan which included the Killerwhale, Shark, Eagle and Grisly Bear.

Page 3

KATS AND SHE-GRISLY IN DISPLAY CASE. The history of this particular sculpture is lost in antiquity. Tradition says that the silver for the eyes and teeth came from the Russians. The hair was obtained from the head of a slave sacrificed at a Potlatch in barbaric times.

Page 6

KOLTEEN OR "KIKSADI" POLE. *Kolteen*, to whose memory this memorial was erected in 1895, was the head of the Wrangell Kiksadi clan, so the pole is often referred to as the "Kiksadi" totem pole. Four stories are suggested by this pole. The top figure is the stylized representation of a sacred mountain up the Stikine river where this band once lived. Beneath that is Frog which is the principal clan symbol of the Kiksadi. A young man of this clan once kicked a frog, fell into a trance and discovered he had kicked a young woman, since the frogs were actually people. Next is *Old Raven* and *Young Raven* facing him, recalling the story wherein Young Raven got light for the earth. At the bottom of the pole is the Killisnoo Beaver whose story is told elsewhere in this volume.

Page 7

THE BEAVER HOUSEPOST. Two houseposts depicting the *Killisnoo Beaver* may be seen in the Saxman Totem Park. Originally pillars in a Tongass Village community house, one depicts *Beaver* holding a bow and an arrow of his manufacture, the other, with his magic spear. (See story)

Page 9

THE SHAMAN SCULPTURE. Known to the Tlingit as an *Ikt*, the shaman or medicine man was a dedicated individual in most instances, convinced of his supernatural powers and relied upon by his people. He attended the sick, ferreted out witches, advised the chief and accompanied war parties. But some were charlatans—crafty, evil and murderous. These gave the entire profession a bad name among the whites.

Page 12

MALE FIGURE WITH SHE-GRISLY AND KATS. Nick Milton whose Indian name is *Kut-u-na-ek* belongs to the Eagle *Taequedi* Clan of the Yakutat Tlingit. From his uncle, *Jim Kat-ee-doo*, he inherited the *Kats* crest shown here with him. This sculpture formerly stood above the entrance of the Brown Bear House (Hootch Hit) in Yakutat. Whenever a Potlatch was to be held in this house, the crest would be displayed out-of-doors above the doorway. This picture was taken in 1952 on the day that Milton consented to let the Territory of Alaska be custodian of his crest.

Page 13

WRANGELL RAVEN POLE. Erected about the same time as the Kolteen pole, the *Wrangell Raven* pole gets its nickname from the prominence of the Ravens carved thereon. It also tells, but more fully, the story of Raven who stole the sunlight for the benefit of mankind. The original keeper of the sun, Raven-at-the-head-of-the-Nass, surmounts the pole, standing on the box that held the sun. Young Raven comes next, carved also as a human being, and beneath him is the daughter to whom he was born. The figure at the bottom is the woman who holds up the earth, called *Hi-yi-shon-a-gu*. She had been Raven's mother in an earlier reincarnation.

Page 16

15

Chapter One

THE TOTEMPOLAR REGION
AND ITS PEOPLE

When one leaves Puget Sound and heads northwestward toward Alaska he almost immediately enters a part of the world known for the past two hundred years as the *Northwest Coast*. This region comprises all of coastal British Columbia and the Alaskan *Panhandle,* more commonly referred to as *Southeastern Alaska.*

This area, roughly a thousand miles long and a hundred miles wide consists of a mainland deeply indented by navigable fiords, inlets, bays and sounds, fringed by countless islands, large and small. So rugged was the land that roads and even trails were practically unknown to the aborigines, the waterways forming a marine highway through a thinly populated one hundred thousand square miles of virgin forest.

This incredibly beautiful land of snow-capped mountains, rock-walled fiords, roaring cataracts and majestic glaciers might well be called the *Totempolar Region* for here was the birthplace and home of those most interesting sculptured cedar monuments erected by an isolated people in a bygone age who had developed an outstanding culture almost single handed.

Due to the presence of a warm oriental ocean current which filters among the islands, the climate is milder than one would expect in these latitudes. Winter temperatures have a mean of thirty-three degrees in the vicinity of Sitka which enjoys a summer maximum of eighty-seven degrees. Warm air coming off the North Pacific Eddy of the Japanese Current and striking the cold air of the coastal mountains gives rise to excessive humidity and is responsible for the almost jungle-like rain forest encountered there. Especially in the islands one finds lichens hanging in festoons from the trees, deep mosses underfoot, ferns and broad-leafed plants growing with tropical luxuriance. But the relation of ocean currents and prevailing winds to lofty coastal mountains that protects this land from extreme cold also cools the summer. There is never a spell of truly hot weather and never the danger of a forest fire. Rainfall, however, varies greatly depending on geographic location. There are spots in the Alaska Panhandle that have as little as twenty inches of rain per annum and others with as much as two hundred and seventy. But water runs off rapidly in a tilted land and floods were unheard of along the shorelines where the people lived in the past. In most cases the modern towns still occupy the sites of prehistoric villages and slides rather than floods are the principal hazard.

The forests which are largely of douglas fir, hemlock and western red cedar at the southern end of the Northwest Coast become, as we reach Alaska, largely western hemlock, Sitka spruce

156
Indian Medicine Man

WP ©
Juneau

SKUN-DOO-OOH, a famous Chilkat Shaman. Physical divergences from the normal such as crossed eyes, hunched backs, a double crown, or red hair were taken as signs of innate occult powers and such individuals were trained from boyhood for the medicine man role. Skun-doo-ooh not only was born with a double crown but had red hair so his destiny was manifest. He became so famous that another shaman, stricken ill, engaged his services for a price of 40 blankets. The suspected witch died of torture and so did the patient a few days later. Skun-doo-ooh was reported to white authority for not refunding the blankets and got a three year term in San Quentin. At Sitka they cut off his hair wherein lay his "power" but it grew out again in prison. There he composed his famous "San Quentin Song" and came back to Alaska more powerful than ever.

find a few red foxes and an occasional coyote, a newcomer to the region. Among the mainland crags one finds mountain goats and the Dall sheep and in the river valleys there are moose presently. They, too, have only recently moved into the region, too late to become a totem animal like the bear and the wolf.

Game birds consist of several varieties of grouse and ptarmigan and such migratory waterfowl as Canada geese, whistling swan, many species of ducks and teal. Songbirds like sparrows, swallows, robins, jays, thrushes, warblers and hummingbirds are common all summer and raise their broods here. Bald eagles, gulls, ravens and jays are the commonest winter birds although grosbeaks, waxwings, chickadees and redpolls seem never to leave, appearing in your yard for a handout whenever in need.

The numberless streams and lakes of this region are generally well-stocked with native cutthroat, dolly varden and rainbow trout. Absent through most of the area are the common panfish like perch, bass, crappie, and catfish. There are no snakes in the totempolar region although toads and newts are common. A true frog (rana pretiosa) has been observed near Wrangell but the "frog" on the totem pole is obviously a toad. Early whites here couldn't distinguish a frog from a toad and their error was taught to the Indians who were also taught that the "raven" was a crow.

Throughout most of the year no insects are to be seen in the region but summer brings mosquitos, gnats and biting flies to plague the fisherman but never in the swarms encountered on the tundra. There are also moths and butterflies and some beetles but hardly enough to keep insectivorous birds around for long.

Marine mammals consist of hair seals, sea lions, whales, killerwhales, the porpoise and, now reported infrequently, the once common sea otter.

and yellow cedar with small stands of red cedar, lodgepole pine and alder, with cottonwood, alder and willow in the river valleys. Underbrush consists mainly of salmonberry, blueberry, currant, red elder, devil's club and buckbrush. Wildflowers appear in great profusion and due to the summer coolness last much longer than one would expect. Among these are fireweed and purple iris, both of which may cover fields acres in extent; the Sitka rose, fairy slippers, several varieties of violets, bluebells, columbine, shooting stars, buttercups, blue geraniums, gentians, primroses and many others.

Land fauna consists of brown, black and grisly bears; wolves, blacktail deer and small furbearers such as mink, marten, beaver, muskrat, land otter and weasel. There are red and flying squirrels, porcupines and marmots. A few wolverine and lynx are seen occasionally, usually when there is a rabbit shortage inland, at which time they come to the coast to prey upon the sparse varying hare population of the coastal river valleys. There one can also

Occasionally fur seals are seen but these are only transients enroute to the Bering Sea.

The principal marine fishes are five species of salmon, halibut, flounder, sole and herring. Also sablefish, pilchard, rockfish, sea perch and eulachon. And unwary sportsfishermen are often plagued by hake, ling, sculpin and tomcod or greenling, blenny or pollock. Sharks which once supplied the natives with a useful "sandpaper" appear in several species but the man-killing species are not present. A small species, the *dogfish*, is an important clan symbol and often appears in the art. Shrimps, prawns and crabs of three commercial species are so plentiful as to be the basis of a thriving industry and clams are packed, commercially. Scallops and a small species of abalone exist in the waters but are still largely unexploited, commercially. All of these with the possible exception of shrimp were important items in the native diet and many of them figured in the art.

Warm waters are responsible for the presence of several marine invertebrates not generally known to exist so far north except by specialists. These are the corals, sea fans, sponges, gorgonia and sea anemones. Summer brings with it great numbers of jellyfish of various types and sizes, colorful starfish as well as sea cucumbers and other odd and interesting sea life.

The birthplace of the totem pole is a sunken land where hilltops become islets, and mountains rise sheer from the water's edge. Its valleys are bays and inlets while its farmland is presently inundated. Some ten thousand years ago glacial ice up to two miles in thickness buried this land, submerging it by its tremendous weight. But now the ice is nearly gone and the land is rebounding as much as an inch a year in some places. Someday there may again be farmland where now there are shallow bays and sounds. The aborigines practiced no agriculture before white men came except to raise small gardens of native tobacco. What soil there is, is rich, and berry and root crops do well. The natives secured their vegetable food by gathering wild berries, crabapples, roots and bulbs, the inner bark of the western hemlock and several varieties of seaweed. Immediately after contact with white men they added to their diet home-grown potatoes and turnips, rhubarb and raspberries, growing them in the beach-side gardens where their tobacco once grew, fertilizing them with decomposed kelp or starfish.

The Native Inhabitants

When the Northwest Coast was first visited by white men some two hundred years ago it was sparsely inhabited, and still is, by five major linguistic groups or tribes, all of whom at some time or other, have carved totem poles or allied monu-

JOHN WALLACE OF HYDABURG. Last of the professional Haida totem-carvers, Johnnie Wallace demonstrated his art before thousands at the World's Fair, Treasure Island, 1939. Shown here with his model of a Haida Community House which once stood at Klinkwan.

Photo by author.

NATIVES OF NOOTKA SOUND,
VANCOUVER ISLAND IN 1778.
From a sketch by Webber in
"Capt. Cook's Voyages."

ments of sculptured cedar commonly called totem poles. The northernmost of these people were the *Tlingit,* known to the Russians in Alaska as *Kolosh.* They occupied all of the costal region, islands as well as mainland, from Yakutat and Klukwan on the north to Cape Fox, south of the present town of Ketchikan, with the exception of the southern half of Prince of Wales Island and Dall Island. These areas had been occupied by invading Haidas some three hundred years ago. Their main seat was the Queen Charlotte Islands off the British Columbia mainland just across Dixon Entrance from Alaska. The Alaskan Haidas were formerly referred to as *Kaigani* from the name of their first settlement in Alaska near the southern tip of Dall Island.

Opposite the Haida, on the mainland between the Nass and the Skeena Rivers and occupying both river valleys, lived the Tsimshian. The Nass branch was known as the *Niska* and those living far inland on the Skeena were called the *Gitksan.* South of the Tsimshian dwelt the *Kwakiutl* who occupied both the mainland and the northeastern part of Vancouver Island. Totem poles of the Kwakiutl may still be seen *in situ* at Alert Bay, a picturesque village on the steamer route to Alaska. A branch of the numerous *Salish* tribe is located on the Bella Coola river and these people are often referred to as *Bella Coolas.* While associated linguistically with the southern Salish of Washington and Southern British Columbia, these Indians had adopted the culture traits of their Northwest Coast neighbors and had become totem pole carvers.

Out on the west coast of Vancouver Island were the *Nootkas* who also were wood carvers, and across the straits of Juan de Fuca at Cape Flattery were the *Makah,* a branch of the Nootka of Wakashan stock. They did not carve and erect tall totem poles but did carve grave figures in the human form and employed carved houseposts in their dwellings.

While the inhabitants of the Totempolar region spoke a half-dozen mutually unintelligible languages, physically they diverged but slightly except in individuals. With the exception of a few Haidas and some others on Vancouver Island who had red hair, all had coarse, straight black hair, black or brown eyes, and a complexion only slightly darker than Europeans. Their stature was somewhat under that of Europeans although they were well-muscled. Legs and arms were relatively short, and feet and hands were small.

In describing the inhabitants of Yakutat in 1787, George Dixon said in part: "they, in general, are about middle size, their limbs straight and well-shaped, but like the rest of the inhabitants we have seen on the coast, are particularly fond of painting their faces with a variety of colors so that it is no easy matter to discover their real complexion; however, we prevailed on one woman, by persuasion, and a trifling present, to wash her face and hands, and the alternation it made in her appearance absolutely surprised us; her countenance had all the cheerful glow of an English milk-maid; and the healthy red which flushed her cheek, was even beautifully contrasted with the whiteness of her neck; her eyes were black and sparkling; her eyebrows the same colour, and most beautifully arched; her forehead so remarkably clear, that the translucent veins were seen meandering even in their minutest branches—in short, she was what would be reckoned handsome even in England. . . ."

A year earlier, in 1786, M. Rollin, Surgeon-major attached to the La Perouse Expedition described the Tlingits at Port des Francais (Lituya Bay) as follows: "These people appear to me to have very little similarity to the Californians; they are taller, stouter, of a more agreeable figure, and a great vivacity of expression; they are also much their superiors in courage and sense. They have rather low foreheads, but more open than that of the Southern Americans; their eyes are black and very animated, their eyebrows much fuller; their nose of the usual size and well-formed, except being a little widened at the extremity; their lips thinner, their mouth moderately large, their teeth fine and very even, their chin and ears very regular.

The women also have an equal advantage over those of the preceding tribes; they have much more mildness in their features and grace in their limbs."

Rollin goes on to deplore the use of the labret, a lip plug which rendered the comliest of women repulsive, stated the general color of the people was

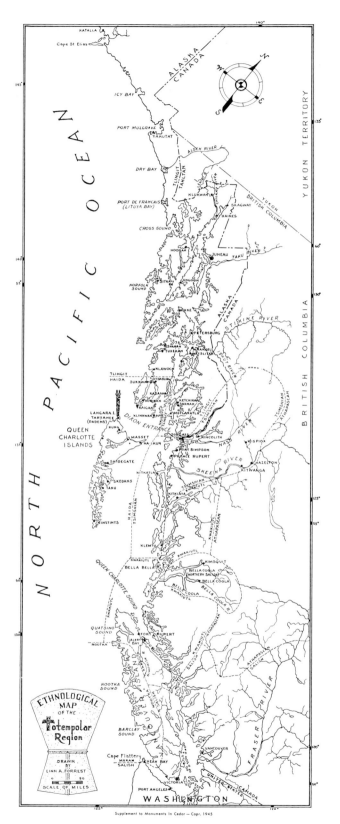

U. S. DEPARTMENT OF INTERIOR
BUREAU OF INDIAN AFFAIRS
WRANGELL INSTITUTE

MODEL "KIKSADI" totem pole made by author's class at Wrangell Institute for presentation to President Roosevelt. Pole was shipped out on first trip of the "Alaska Clipper" in 1940; now reposes in the Hyde Park Museum.

Photo by author.

olive, that their hair was neither as black or coarse as that of South Americans and that chestnut colored hair was by no means infrequent among them.

Kotzebue, who visited Sitka in 1825, was not so complimentary yet can hardly be relied upon since his description is filled with obvious inaccuracies and exaggerations. For instance, he charged them with "head-flattening," a practice never indulged in by any Alaska natives. In describing the labrets worn in the lips of the Tlingit and Haida women, Kotzebue gives free rain to his vivid imagination: "In running, the lips flap up and down so as to knock sometimes against the chin and sometimes against the nose. Upon the continent, the kaluga (labret) is worn still larger, and the female who can cover her whole face with her under-lip passes for the most perfect beauty. . . ."

John Meares describes the Nootkas on the west coast of Vancouver Island whom he visited in 1788 as follows: "In their exterior form they have not the symmetry or elegance which is found in many other Indian nations. Their limbs, though stout and athletic, are crooked and ill-shaped; their skin, when cleansed of filth and ochre, is white, and we have seen some women, when in a state of cleanliness, which, however, was by no means a common sight, and obtained with difficulty, who not only possessed the fair complexion of Europe, but features that would have attracted notice for their deli-

cacy and beauty, in those parts of the world where the qualities of the human form are best understood . . . their hair, like that of the men, is black; their eyes are of the same color; and, in their exterior appearance, they are not to be immediately distinguished from the men. In their characters they are reserved and chaste; and examples of loose and immodest conduct were very rare among them."

Camille de Roquefeuil, a French navigator who visited the Northwest Coast in 1817 with the object of reviving French trade which had been almost annihiliated by the Revolution, made many interesting observations of the people he saw there. Speaking of the inhabitants of "Nitinat" described as a village on Berkeley Sound several leagues south of Nootka, he said, "We saw several men and a greater number of women, whose complexion differed from white only by a tinge of pale yellow. Some young people, of both sexes, had a colour, and many children would have been thought pretty in Europe. The greater number of the Indians have black hair, the remainder a light red, all wear the hair long, and the women comb it carefully, and divide it over the middle of the forehead. Both sexes dress the same as at Nootka, with this difference, that the women wear under their other garments a kind of apron of bark, not woven, but only fastened to a girdle. We saw many well-made women with good arms, but in general, very ugly hands. On the whole they are better looking than the women of Nootka, though there is something harsher in their countenances, chiefly owing to their narrow foreheads, which are wrinkled at an early age. We saw only three or four who in Europe would have any pretensions to beauty. One of them was the wife of Cia, who had received us hospitably; another, the wife of a great chief, was almost white; she had large black eyes, regular features, a fine countenance, and much propriety and dignity in her manners. The women and girls appeared as modest as those of Nootka, and still more reserved."

The tradition of "red-headed natives in hula skirts" on the Northwest Coast has generally been attributed to the Haidas, among whom there has always been a fair percentage of red-heads but Roquefeuil places them several hundred miles farther south on Vancouver Island rather than in the Queen Charlottes. Red hair is still quite common among the Kaigani Haidas now centering in Alaska at Hydaburg.

Captain George Dixon visited the Queen Charlotte Islands in 1787 and described the Haidas as follows: "The people in general are about the middle size, their limbs straight, and tolerable well-shaped; many of the older people are rather lean, but I never saw one person who could be called corpulent amongst them; both sexes are remarkably distinguished by high prominent cheek bones and small eyes. . . . In regard to their complexion, it is no easy matter to determine what cast that is; but if I may judge from the few people I saw tolerably clean, these Indians are very little darker than the Europeans in general."

He remarked that the hair of both sexes was long and black, that the young men pluck out their beards but that in advanced years men had beards all over the chin and some had moustaches.

Marchand also described the Haidas of Queen Charlotte Islands whom he visited in 1791. He found them not differing materially in stature from Europeans, better proportioned and better formed than the Sitkans and without the gloomy and wild look of the latter. Their color he found did not differ from that of Frenchmen, and several were less swarthy "than the inhabitants of our country places."

Soap was unknown on this coast at that time yet Surgeon Roblet testified that communication with Europeans had already produced remarkable changes, both in the toilet and in their customs.

Speaking of the young Haida women, Roblet says: "They carefully comb their fine locks; they frequently wash themselves, and suffer on their bodies no hair on any other part than the head. When their cheeks are cleaned and stripped of the

coat which is foreign to them, their natural bloom is discovered: it is not roses scattered on lilies, but still it is roses. The eyes which, for a long time past, were saddened by the color of night spread over the

INDIAN POLICEMAN. Shortly after the purchase of Alaska in 1867, Indian police were appointed to help keep their tribesmen in line. Here, Willie Peters of Juneau models the police uniform of his illustrious ancestor, Chief Kowee.

CHIEF ANATLAHASH II. Better known in Juneau as Jimmie Fox, the present Taku Chief, is the nephew of Chief Anatlahash who was the head Taku Indian when Juneau was founded. Jimmie has an extensive tribal wardrobe and has appeared publicly in several different tribal costumes. Once, for an official visit to the Great White Chief in Washington, D.C., he provided himself with a silk topper, striped trousers and cutaway coat. Well past 90 and blind, he has retired from social life.

dark faces of the American women of the coast, dwelt with pleasure on the colour of youth. The French began to find them passable; and we imagine that they ended by finding them pretty."

Sir George Simpson, travelling northward in 1842, gives a pretty picture of the Northern Salish whom he saw on the mainland opposite Cape Mudge, Vancouver Island: "In the fleet that swarmed around us we observed two peculiarly neat canoes, with fourteen paddles each, which savoured very strongly of honeymoon. Each carried a young couple, who, both in dress and demeanour, were evidently a newly-married pair, the gentlemen, with their 'arms around their dearies O', were lavishing their little attentions on the ladies, to the obvious satisfaction of both parties. The brides were young and pretty, tastefully decked out with beads, bracelets, anklets, and various ornaments in their hair, and, above all, with blankets so sweet, and sound and clean, that they could not be otherwise than new. The bridegrooms were smart, active, handsome fellows, all as fine as a holiday, and more particularly proud of their turbans of white calico." Such were the natives of the Northwest Coast when white men found them.

»»»→

POTLATCHERS AT SITKA. Around the turn of the century, Alaska's Tlingit Indians, newly prosperous from Gold Rush earnings, staged a cultural revival that almost rivaled that of the days of sea-otter prosperity. Potlatches were held and much native finery was made and displayed. But it was lost on the journalists of the day who probably weren't even invited. Great things were accomplished, socially, by the Indians but the newspapers only reported "much noise and great excitement at the *Ranche*" if they mentioned it at all.

Case & Draper (after Merrill).

CHILKATS IN DANCING CUSTOMS AT SITKA POTLATCH   COPYRIGHT DEC. 23, 1904.
                                                   BY CASE & DRAPER.

GROUP OF HAIDAS AT VILLAGE OF KLINKWAN. The man at the right with the Chilkat blanket over his lap was the carver of the "Old Witch" totem pole which formerly stood in Sukkwan and now stands beside the library in Juneau. His son was John Wallace, another famous Haida carver, who as a boy helped his father carve the so-called "Old Witch" totem pole. (See story of Mother-in-law trouble.)

KOW-ISH-TE (CHIEF SHAKES V) LYING IN STATE. Taken in 1878 in Fort Wrangell, this photo shows Chief Shakes V lying in state surrounded by the symbols of his tribe and clan. Kow-ish-te, who became Shakes V upon the death of his uncle, was Chief when the Russians came to build Redoubt St. Dionysius in 1833, was Chief when the British built Fort Stikine during the period of their lease, and was still Chief when the U.S. purchased Alaska and constructed Fort Wrangell. The Killer Whale staff which was his sceptre, and the sceptre of all the Shakes dynasty, is shown at his right.

A GRAVE TOTEM. Originally this female grisly bear sat in the cemetery of old *Sukkwan,* near the present village of Hydaburg, flanked by a pair of cubs, all three of which held salmon in their paws. But a trader purchased the cubs and provided marble slabs for the graves they watched over. Now the empty hands of the mother bear symbolize her bereavement.

Photo by the author.

CHIEF ANATLAHASH. This was the famous and revered Taku Chief who held sway over his tribe in the Juneau-Douglas area during the early days of discovery and gold-mining along Gastineau Channel. One of the physical traits of these people noted by the earliest explorers who called them *primitive whites* was their heavy beards, which in youth, they plucked out with muscle-shell tweezers.

28

Chapter Two

ORIGIN OF THE TOTEM POLE

Those who have pondered the origin of the Northwest Coast totem pole and its allies may be regarded as occupying two opposing schools of thought: those who hold that the totem pole is post-European, and those who consider it to be prehistoric. The leading exponent of the first group is the eminent Canadian anthropologist, Dr. Marius Barbeau, and of the second, perhaps Wolfgang Paalen. Both have been over the ground and are well-equipped to speak on the subject. Their books and papers on the subject are listed in the accompanying bibliography.

What has contributed most to the highly divergent views of these authorities is a seeming paradox presented by the totem poles themselves for, whereas most historical evidence points to a recent development of these colossal monuments, students of primitive art are unanimous in their belief that the art style therein employed is one of the truly great art styles of all time and therefore could not possibly be of recent origin. Of it, Paalen has this to say: "all objects of totem art bear the seal of the same severe and powerful rhythm that ordered the existence of these peoples. The surface of a box sufficed for the inscription of compositions of a marvelous richness; many of the achievements of their art and crafts that cannot even be enumerated here have not been surpassed in any other culture."

Of the totem pole itself, the Haidas of the Queen Charlotte Islands brought it to its fullest development. The first heraldic pole known to science was the one seen on Langara Island, Q.C. I., in 1791 recorded in a sketch in Bartlett's Journal of the same year. In Cook's Third Voyage, published in 1785, there appears a sketch of the interior of a Nootka house featuring carved interior house pillars; in *Malaspina's Voyage Around the World 1789-94*, appears a plate showing monumental sculptured mortuaries at Yakutat Bay. Thus, it may be seen that before the end of the 18th century monumental carvings in cedar were to be encountered along a coastal expanse of a thousand miles. Presuming the art had its inception with the Haida as is quite generally conceded, and considering its spread of roughly 500 miles north and south by 1800, it becomes most difficult to accept as post-European, especially when we recall that Alaska was discovered as late as 1741, and was not occupied until 1799 when the Russians returned to settle Sitka. Nootka, on Vancouver Island, had been occupied by the Spanish out of Mexico in 1790. In the generation preceding 1800 and for at least a generation after that date, the only contact the totem-carving people had with Europeans, excepting at Nootka and Sitka, was with the northwest fur traders who, for safety, traded under sail, mid-channel. Few of these traders

TLINGIT OIL BOWL. While the Tlingit usually carved their oil bowls in the form of a seal, the sleeping sea otter motif was also popular. Seal oil or eulachon grease served as butter and at state feasts food was dipped in oil served in individual bowls such as this. The wood employed was alder since it imparted no taste or odor to the food. Inlay is of abalone and skeletal whale bone.

Alaska State Museum Collection.

ever saw the winter villages of the Indians so they did not know if totem poles were in them, and acculturation was at a minimum.

There is plenty evidence that totem poles had their origin right where they were found. Archaeological evidence indicates that these people were not only marine hunters and fishermen but rain foresters, as well. Tall, easily worked cedar was felled with stone implements for the making of building timbers and planks and huge dugout canoes. When the culture had advanced to the stage where public records were in demand, here was ready material. Men are inspired by the tall majesty of trees like the giants that grew on the Northwest Coast. Lofty eminences have always inspired men the world over, be they natural or man-made. Snow-clad mountain peaks became, in imagination, the abode of benign gods; fiery, smoking volcanic cones, those of malign spirits. Monoliths, buttes and other high natural formations have had especial significance attached to them in mythology and in lore. Where they did not exist in nature, man has made them in imitation—pyramids, obelisks, towers, spires and totem poles to name a few. Then, perhaps only as an afterthought, he has put them to work as tombs, lookouts, bell towers, beacons or public records.

The dwellers on the Northwest Coast were no exception. Man settled there quite recently, geo-

logically speaking, especially since the deglaciation of the region has only in the past 700 or 800 years uncovered and rendered habitable enough of the good earth to accommodate the canoes and bark huts of an early band of gatherers.

The cycle of occupation may have been something like this: toward the end of the latest glaciation on the Northwest Coast the confluent glaciers were discharging many miles to sea and there was no beach land as yet uncovered. But, as the recession of the ice set in and the glacier faces retreated, immense sand and gravel banks were exposed and fresh water rivulets and lakes formed. Then schools of salmon, searching for spawning beds, moved into these ideal regions as soon as they appeared. There they carried on the reproductive cycle repeated to this day in the still-enlarging area. Soon the bears, ravens and eagles discovered the salmon there and at once took up permanent abode close to this never-failing food supply. At length man appeared and, whether nomad or castaway, decided that this was the place and roved no more.

Meanwhile, a forest of spruce was springing up in the barren gravel, and in its early humus was nurtured a secondary forest of hemlock and red cedar. Along the streams appeared willows, alders and cottonwood trees from seeds wind or stream borne from the interior. All this could have happened within the life span of a man. All of it has happened on a reduced scale at the face of Mendenhall glacier near Juneau in a single decade (1941-51).

Everywhere were salmon-eaters, but the greatest salmon-eater of all was man. Man took as his first totems in this region, the raven and the eagle with which he had reasons to identify himself. Other salmon-eaters became his clan symbols to figure later in the plastic art of the region. Among these were the black and brown or grisly bear; the sea-lion and the killerwhale. The deer, the moose and the porcupine arrived too late to achieve any prominence in the art, and the fox and the lynx are missing for the same reason.

When the time came for man to exalt his totem bird or animal and to advertize his own mythical lineage, what better inspiration did he need than this same eagle or raven perched majestically on a tree top surveying its new-found domain and speculating, perhaps, on these strange new animals that used fire and also relished salmon?

Whether it was an eagle or a raven perching on a stump; or a bear up a tree, or merely standing, man-like, on its hind legs, the original inspiration for a totemic monument could have been any one

DUK-TOOTHL. This bone pendent was unearthed by foxes on a small island near the village of Kake. It depicts Duk-toothl, a culture hero who rose from a despised weakling to chieftainship. (See Story.) He is shown here standing on an off-shore rock which appears as an inverted hawk's head. His upper arms are in the form of sea lions and a bird is emerging from his mouth. Faces form his knee joints, and an animal head covers his chest. Sea lion entrails form his headdress and drape to the base. Carvings like this of bone, stone and ivory were later made of cedar in enormous versions to form the pillars of community houses. Photo by the author.

of them. For we know that the earliest and simplest totem poles, as well as the commonest, were nothing more than a bare pole surmounted by a totem bird or animal, generally a raven, an eagle, or a bear. The wolf came later from the mainland. And the beautifully sculptured highly ornate poles found in our parks are certainly post-European.

Who these first settlers were has not been established. Boas and other anthropologists agree that in the present inhabitants, two racial strains are blended. One is Athapascan in origin as is well-documented in the lore of these nomads who have many tales of their descent to the coast down raging rivers and under the glaciers, migrating from the hinterland to the sea. The other, whom the Athapascans found when they reached the beach, appears to be a Mongol from north Asia. One is tempted to think of this element as a shipwrecked band of fairly modern men, or maritime nomads, arriving with empty hands and empty pockets, but carrying in their minds a memory of a great and

KAIGANI TOTEMS. Situated near the southern tip of Dall Island, Kaigani village was the first seat of the Haida Indians in Alaska when they migrated from the Queen Charlotte Islands more than 200 years ago. Here in 1794 a white sea captain and his crew planed, painted and erected a totem pole to ingratiate themselves with the chief and to aid the fur trade. The poles shown here sprouting trees could well have dated from that day.

Photo by Davidson.

OLD HOUSE PILLARS FROM YAKUTAT. Jim Kat-ee-doo, chief of the Yakutat Ta-quo-adi, is here shown standing beside the house pillars from *Toosch Hit,* or Mud Shark House. The mud shark clan symbol is shown at the base of each pillar. The upper figures are brown bear, eagle, and the fisherman who caught the legendary mud shark.

civilized past. Much more digging must be done before anything about this man can be established, but from the meager contents of his shallow middens, this Asiatic had a rough time of it in a land of plenty until discovered by Europeans and again brought into contact with civilization.

So far, his middens have revealed no flaked implements; his arrows were tipped with mussel shell or bone; he had no knowledge of the toggle-type harpoon or the bow-drill of the Eskimo; his own bone creations were as crude and clumsy as those any New Yorker might make today were he shipwrecked in the same spot under similar conditions. If this maroon had ever known the use of metal tools, the smelting of metal from the ore was beyond his ability for the ores of both copper and iron were nearby. But he appreciated the qualities of iron and copper and sought it on the beaches in wreckage that probably had its origin in the Orient.

Even without metal tools these people could ply their arts and did. Bone, antler, and ivory can be worked with nephrite, a material they had; hardwood such as maple, alder and crabapple yield easily to tools of shell or beaver teeth. But, odd as it may seem, soft, red cedar cannot be carved successfully with any of these materials. Very soft wood such as western red cedar must be worked with thin, razor-sharp blades since a blunt blade will only crush it. Metal was so scarce that only a few of the most powerful chief had it, or the thin imported jade blades, so only they could boast the fine community houses with heraldic columns before them, fashioned from the local red cedar.

The *Golden Age* of the totem pole could not and did not begin until northwest traders introduced the recently-adopted iron adze or "toe" from Polynesia in wholesale lots. A fortunate combination of new iron tools, a new-rich gentry based on the sea-

otter trade and an overwhelming ambition to out-do the old aristocracy brought about a renaissance both in the art and literature of the Northwest Coast. For now professional carvers were imported from distant tribes or villages and retained at fancy prices to carve greatly-enlarged versions of the posts that once stood indoors. Social-climbing clansmen searched the oral literature even of neighboring linguistic groups for totem pole motifs to advertize a fictitious lineage or at least one based on mythology. So it was that the period roughly between 1830 and 1880 saw the construction of the largest houses and the finest totem poles ever to be seen on the Northwest Coast. A closely following combination of schoolbooks and Bibles, an outlawed *potlatch,* and the ending of slavery, plus the coming of the modern salmon cannery spelled doom to the native community house and totem pole and brought to an untimely end the pursuit of the native arts and literature.

Barbeau believes that totem poles derive from three contributing sources: carved house posts, graveyard figures common along the coast to Bering Strait, and also in Siberia and Japan, and miniature carvings of stone, ivory, and wood which "show that at least some of the stylistic devices of the native carvers were older than the totem poles and presumably went back to Asiatic prototypes."

Although Barbeau does not elaborate, he probably was thinking of such portable objects as sha-

CEREMONIAL FOOD TRAY. The four sides of this tray are made from one yew-wood board, kerfed, steamed, and bent into position. The bottom is pegged to the sides with hard-wood pegs. The design is carved in low relief, smoothed with sharkskin, stained and polished. Such trays were used at ceremonial dinners and when stored were protected by slip covers of woven cedar matting. Although of Haida manufacture, this tray was collected in Tlingit territory at Dyea in 1907 by Thomas Riggs who later became Governor of Alaska. He presented it to the Territorial Museum of which he was the father.

man's charms, chief's staffs, batons, ladle handles, and canes, any of which could be scaled to totem dimensions when necessity demanded.

Dawson said: "A carved stick is sometime held in the hand in dancing, and struck upon the floor in time with the motion of the feet. Several of those which I have seen are about five feet in length, and are carved much in the style of the posts which are set up in front of the houses. Figures of men and conventionalized representations of animals appear to be seated one above another up the length of the stick."

It is common knowledge in Wrangell that the shorter of the two Kadashan totem poles was the exact replica of a cane presented to Kadashan by a Haida chief many years ago. The knob-like eagle head surmounting the pole verifies its lowly origin.

A former Chilkat totem pole carver, Charley Tagcook, carved both totem poles and chief's staffs from the same model. One in the Alaska State Museum that he carved is represented to be a replica of the staff of Chief Donnawok of the Yindustucki Chilkats. It has the slightly flaring base of a totem pole and would scale into one without alteration. Several other staffs and canes in the museum collection suggest totem poles. In his book, Niblack figures many canes, wands, and batons equally reminiscent of totem poles. Still earlier is a shaman's charm in the writer's collection. This is a beautifully-carved bone pendant bearing the likeness of *Duk-duthl* or *Kahasi*, a culture hero with two names. It was unearthed by foxes on Hare Island

HAIDA HOUSE. This wolfish face represents the head of Wasgo, who according to some accounts had a "head like a house." The medallion-like faces represent the young man who killed the monster, got into its skin and assumed its powers. Charlie Edensaw was also a silversmith and employed the silversmith's techniques in his stone work. Two of the gargoyles are missing. The house was carved sometime prior to 1890.

Photo by Bob DeArmond.

HAIDA HOUSE. This miniature argillite community house is believed to have been carved by Charlie Edensaw of Masset, dean of the Haida carvers and silversmiths. The roof decorations are sea lions and the gargoyle-like rafter tips represent the head of Wasgo. Alaska State Museum collection.

Photo by Bob DeArmond.

near Kake in 1926. Although it illustrates a well-known hero story of the Northwest Coast and carries all the stylistic devices of totem art, the physiognomy is definitely Asiatic, the craftsmanship excellent. It would scale ideally into an interior house pillar.

Among other suspected ancestors of the ornate totem pole are the black argillite *story masters* of the Haidas. Although Paalen stigmatizes them as a representation of the "decadent stage at which a great art loses its *raison d'etre* and degenerates to trifles" he bends enough to credit them with being "at times beautiful and of great craftsmanly perfection."

Argillite carvings, often referred to as "slate" appeared around 1820 after white men searching for coal on Skidegate Inlet, Queen Charlotte Islands, discovered the stone of which they are made. Sea otters were getting scarce and the Haidas needed something new for dollar exchange. The easily carved carbonacous shalestone was the answer. For the next hundred years highly skilled artists produced platters, figurines, pipes, flutes and model totem poles of argillite for a ready market. Since the ornate totem poles of the same period are nothing more than a totem combined with a *story* for decoration, the Haida story-master of argillite must be taken into account whenever the ancestors of ornate totem poles are considered.

Contemporary with argillite carvings were the

STONE STORYMASTERS OF THE HAIDA. These Haidite (Queen Charlotte black argillite) carvings were the inspiration of the later tall totem poles in red cedar and set the art style for the entire Northwest Coast. Wickersham Collection.
Photo by Winter & Pond.

decorative spoon or ladle handles of the Haida and Tsimshian. These often had a bowl of sheep horn and a handle of black mountain goat horn riveted on. Like many other small carvings of these people, spoon handles could also have been inspiration for tall totem poles. At least the craftsmanship equalled that of the argillite carvings and both surpassed anything being done in wood at the time.

Other elements that may have entered the picture and influenced the art style of the Northwest Coast were various objects cast up by the sea. Authentic records of junks cast on these shores are well known. A story in the Haida literature tells of a totem pole that drifted to their shores, water-logged, and was discovered by them beneath the surface. Some believe that it was the inspiration for their first totem pole.

Today and for hundreds of years perhaps, favored spots from the Queen Charlotte Islands to Prince William Sound and beyond, receive large amounts of flotsam presumably from the Orient and the islands of the Pacific. Included in the drift are exotic woods, sections of bamboo and coconuts. It also consists of wreckage bearing iron and copper spikes which account for the metal tools possessed by the Indians and observed by Cook and Dixon. In 1947, a carved wooden figurine of Japanese origin drifted ashore near Cape Muzon on Dall Island and was recovered by a Haida fisherman who still has it in his possession. It appears to be a stylized figure of a Japanese warrior about one foot long and still bore traces of its original lacquer. In 1949, another figurine about the same size came ashore near Kodiak on Long Island and was found by a native boy. It was identified as a Japanese copy of a Chinese original. Neither of these carvings have anything in common with totem art as we know it today, although one bears a startling resemblance to some early Aleut masks from the Shumagin Islands now in the Alaska State Museum. Nevertheless, their appearance on Northwest Coast beaches demonstrates how easily art objects and therefore art styles may be introduced to a people thousands of miles from the originators with no other intermediary but the wide ocean.

It is apparent that as the matter stands, we have many theories but little evidence concerning the origin of totem poles or the people who made them. However, we do have the writings of men who were on the Northwest Coast from 1774 to the present and to them we turn for the only record there is.

CHINESE CAMPHORWOOD CHESTS. Chests like these were first imported to Alaska by a Yankee in 1799. Made of camphorwood in Canton, China, they were covered with split pigskin painted red, green, blue or black and studded with brass tacks. A few like the one on top were brass-bound but lacked the leather cover. Indians bought them in great numbers to take the place of their own bentwood cedar boxes. Mostly they were used for storage of ceremonial finery, but some became receptacles for the ashes of the cremated dead.
Photographed in Kake about 1930 by the author.

Chapter Three

THE ANTIQUITY OF THE TOTEM POLE

Totem poles, *in situ*, are bound to give the impression of great age. This is due largely to the presence even today of many standing totem poles in deserted village sites, too rotten to be repaired or even moved—lichen-covered, mossy, leaning—seemingly older than the pyramids. The impression they give is further borne out by the Indians when questioned about these relics of the past. They either profess to know nothing about them or their stories about them are at such variance that no two accounts of any particular pole seem to coincide.

That totem poles, however dilapidated, are not necessarily of great age, certainly not prehistoric, may be noted in the case of New Tongass village on Tongass Island. Here the poles appear to be as ancient as any on the Northwest Coast, yet we know positively that none were carved before 1867, the year the Indians got permission to build their new village under protection of the American guns at Fort Tongass which also was established that year. At this site, the *Lincoln* totem pole was falling apart at the age of fifty years; it was beyond all repair at the age of seventy. Partly responsible for this, other than the rigors of climate, is the fact that, once erected, the finest totem poles were never repaired or repainted by the men who put them up. This was because, under their social system, these Indians could not engage in repairs except with great formality and expense for which no new honors accrued to the owner. Economically and socially, it was smarter to erect a new pole.

In questioning natives about the totem poles in their neighborhood, one is generally disappointed with the results. The younger Indians have not been taught the meaning of the poles and older tribesmen are generally reluctant to discuss tribal matters with outsiders. But another reason is that the Indians of the Northwest Coast recognized a property right in stories as well as in songs and dances. In other words, one could not sing a song which was the property of another, or dance his dance or tell his story. These were prerogatives reserved for exercise on social occasions. A friendly Indian might go so far as to advise one to whom he should go to have the story told even though he knew the story himself, for to tell it would be to infringe upon the prerogatives of his neighbor.

All things considered, it becomes apparent that our only hope of establishing the age of totem poles rests in the accounts given us by the first European visitors to these shores.

Alexei Chirikof landed men near Sitka in 1741 but none were every heard of again hence left no record of what was seen there on that great voyage of discovery. Vitus Bering did little better.

35

KADISHAN TOTEM POLES. When dry rot put the originals beyond repair, these duplicates were carved and erected on Shakes Island. Specially treated, they should endure a hundred years.

Photo by author.

Touching at Cape St. Elias some thirty-six hours after Chirikof had sighted land, he allowed a watering party only six hours ashore. They made no mention of having seen strange monuments there but did report having found huts made of smooth boards, in some places carved. At least they established that wood-carvers dwelt on the Northwest Coast before the coming of white men.

The next voyage into the Totempolar Region was that of the Spaniard, Juan Perez, in 1774. He got as far as Cape Muzon on Dall Island but did not land, unfortunately. But the following year the pilot, Maurelle, who was with Quadra wrote of a landing at Sitka. He did not mention totem poles of any types being seen at Sitka at that time so it is safe to assume there were none there prior to 1775. This date, however, marks the beginning of an extensive trade on this coast between the natives and Spanish, French, English, Russian and American traders and explorers. The principal item desired by these Indians in trade for their furs was iron, either implement or bar. It is natural, then, that whatever crafts that had formerly been carried on by the use of stone tools would be greatly accelerated with the introduction of steel.

As mentioned earlier, iron and copper were not unknown to these people. A little may have reached them through trade with other Indians in contact with white men. But so much iron came to them in wreckage that the Haidas believed *iron logs* found on their beaches was the natural source of all iron. These logs were constantly sought for and were recognized by the stains of the metal. Black stains signified iron and green stains, copper. Stained logs were burned to recover the metal they contained. Iron was called *yaatz* by the Haidas and their first name for white men was *yaatz haada* or *iron people* because these pale strangers had such great quantities of this precious metal when first encountered on their ships.

Captain James Cook who visited Nootka on the West Coast of Vancouver Island in 1778 testifies to the extensive use of iron at that early date. I quote him directly: "Their great dexterity in works of wood may, in some measure be ascribed to the assistance they receive from iron tools, for, as far as we know, they use no other; at least we saw only one chisel of bone. And though, originally their tools must have been of different materials, it is not improbable that many of their improvements have been made since they acquired a knowledge of that metal, which now is universally used in their various wooden works. The chisel and the knife are the only forms, as far as we saw, that iron assumes amongst them. The chisel is a long flat piece, fitted into a handle of wood. A stone serves for a mallet, and a piece of fish-skin for a polisher. I have seen some of these chisels that were eight or ten inches long, and three or four inches broad but in general they were smaller. The knives are of various sizes; some very large; and their blades are crooked, somewhat like our pruning-knife; but the edge is on the back or convex part. Most of them that we saw were about the breadth and thickness of an iron hoop; and their singular form marks that they are not of European make. Probably, they are imitations of their own original instruments, used for the same purposes. They sharpen these iron tools upon a coarse slate whetstone and likewise keep the whole instrument constantly bright."

The French explorer, Juan La Perouse, who spent considerable time at Lituya Bay in 1786 described the natives there at length, and his artist drew sketches of them and their boats and houses. But nowhere does he mention or show sketches of totem poles from which we must conclude that there were none there at that time.

George Dixon and Matthew Portlock who were on the Northwest Coast in 1787 had much the same experience. Dixon explored and named the Queen Charlotte Islands. He saw many of the inhabitants and collected a rich harvest of sea otter skins but apparently saw no totem poles of any kind. In Dixon's case it is not conclusive that there were no totem poles there for he purposely avoided the villages, fearing attack. All of his trading was done between boat parties from his ship and canoe parties of Haidas who went out from hidden villages to barter.

A most significant fact, however, is that in trading for sea otter pelts, the item most in demand by the natives was the *toe* or *towe*. This word, which is Polynesian in origin, means adze in Tahiti and is used entirely for *adze* by Dixon and other traders on the Northwest Coast. In trading with the Haidas,

INTERIOR HOUSE PILLARS AT NOOTKA IN 1778. From a sketch by Webber in "Capt. Cook's Voyages."

JOHN MUIR'S SKETCH. John Muir sketched this Bear Totem at Kotslitan (Old Wrangell) in 1879 when its condition indicated it was at least fifty years old. When photographed by the author in 1940 it was easily the oldest standing pole in Alaska.

(Sketch from John Muir's Alaska Notebook, Sierra Club Bulletin, Vol. X)

THE BEAR TOTEM OF KOTSLITAN. This is the mortuary pole sketched by John Muir in 1879 as it appeared sixty years later. It is the only totem pole standing at Kotslitan, the village that was abandoned a hundred years ago, when the Russians built their fort at Wrangell.

Photo by author.

toes were desired to the exclusion of any other trade goods in some instances; they were even given to children for presents.

Since the adze is the principal tool used in carving totem poles as well as in making house planks and canoes, considerable impetus must have been given to woodworking of all kinds at this time for now almost anyone could have tools that once were possessed only by the wealthiest chiefs. In the Queen Charlotte Islands the stone age had ended over night.

John Meares, in his "Voyages to the Northwest Coast of America" published in London in 1790 hinted strongly of the existence of totems of some

sort in the Queen Charlotte Islands. On page 367 occurs this passage, ". . . and the great wooden images of Tartanee bore East, one quarter North; the village on the opposite shore bearing South half West. This harbor is in the latitude of 54 degrees 18 minute N. and longitude 227 degrees six minutes East. . . ."

Meares was no doubt referring to exterior house posts or heraldic totem poles at a Haida village on Langara Island just off the Northwest tip of Graham Island. Since this was on the year following Dixon's visit to these islands, it is reasonable to conclude they were there but passed unobserved by Dixon's men, due, no doubt, to their reluctance if not orders, to go near the native village where in those days they might well be captured and held for ransom.

This same Haida village on Langara or North Island was described by Etienne Marchand in his "A Voyage Round the World 1790-92." He gives perhaps the first good description of a Haida family or heraldic pole such as they erected against the front of their houses and which served as doorways through which they entered their ornate habitations.

On page 401, he says, "This opening is made in the thickness of a large trunk of a tree which rises perpendicularly in the middle of one of the fronts of the habitation, and occupies the whole of its height; it imitates the form of a gaping human mouth, or rather that of a beast, and it is surmounted by a hooked nose, about two feet in length, proportional in point of size, to the monstrous face to which it belongs . . . over the door is seen the figure of a man carved in the attitude of a child in the womb, and remarkable for the extreme smallness of the parts which characterize his sex; and above this figure rises a gigantic statue of a man erect, which terminates the sculpture and the decoration of the portal; the head of this statue is dressed with a cap in the form of a sugar loaf, the height of which is almost equal to that of the figure itself. On the parts of the surface which are not occupied by the capital subjects, are interspersed carved figures of frogs or toads, lizards and other

animals, the arms, legs, thighs and other parts of the human body. . . ."

Marchand added that these totems were of lively red, black and apple green and remarked that the houses across the channel, that is, on Graham Island, had no poles.

The Alaska or *Kaigani* Haidas are descended from a group that originally lived on Langara Island and crossed Dixon's Entrance to Dall Island about three hundred years ago. It is perhaps they who introduced the totem pole to Alaska, if not to the world. These are the people who have the legend to the effect that the first totem pole drifted ashore on Langara Island from parts unknown, providing them with a model from which all later totem poles are believed by them to have originated. It is at least significant that totem poles were observed at this spot when they were still unreported by seamen who visited all the other native settlements of any importance on the Coast.

In his article, "A Yankee Trader on the Northwest Coast, 1791-1795" in Vol. XXI, No. 2 of the Washington Historical Quarterly, Judge F. W. Howay relates the exploits of Captain Roberts of the *Jefferson*. While at *Kaigani*, a Haida village on Dall Island in 1794, the Captain had occasion to assist in making and erecting a totem pole. I quote: "To ingratiate themselves and to aid the trade, the Captain with the carpenter and some of the crew went to the village to plane and smooth a totem

MORTUARY POLE AT YAKUTAT IN 1792. From an artist's sketch appearing in Malaspina's "Viaje Alrededor Del Mundo, 1789-1794." (See Text.)

TONGASS VILLAGE. This view of Tongass Village taken in 1889 shows at the extreme right, the totem pole which was purloined ten years later by members of a *Goodwill* touring party from Seattle. The theft was observed by an old woman who reported it to fellow tribesmen returning to the village after being absent, fishing. Two war canoes were manned and dispatched to Seattle to bring back the monument but they returned to Alaska loaded only with promises of restitution and some cash. The thieves were fined $1,000 and the pole was subsequently set up in Pioneer Square where it remained until it was rotted beyond repair at which time it was duplicated by Tlingit carvers in Ketchikan and presented to the City of Seattle as an Alaskan *Goodwill* gesture. A passenger who aided in snatching the pole in 1899 was alive in Orlando, Florida in 1960. He still had a halibut hook he liberated from a cabin in the village at that time.

pole. The next day they returned with two spare top-masts and the necessary tackle to raise the pole and set it in position."

Later, Cunneah, the chief, asked Captain Roberts to have the pole painted, which he did. Some days later at Cunneah's request, men were sent to raise and place a carved figure on the top of the totem pole, the figure resembling a toad.

The first good description of a Tlingit mortuary pole comes from the Italian, Don Alexandro Malaspina, in the service of Spain, who saw several at Yakutat in 1792. In his book "Voyage Round the World 1789-94" is a drawing of a large bear totem holding in its paws a box containing ashes of the dead. His description follows: "We do not know whether the colossal monster which occupies the foreground is an idol or merely a frightful record of the destructive nature of death, but the fact that in its vicinity are various pyres on which bodies have been cremated inclines us to the first idea. In a casket which lay beneath its claws or hands was a bowl-shaped basket, a European hat, an otter skin and a piece of board. The height of the monster was no less than ten and a half feet (French). The whole was of pine wood and the ornaments on the casket were of shells embedded in the same wood. The colouring was of red ochre with the exception of

the teeth, the claws and the upper parts of the head which were painted black and white. In the upper chamber of the two sepulchral deposits were two baskets, one greater than the other, the contents covered with loose boards, containing a basket with some calcined bones, broken up very small so that it was scarcely possible to distinguish between the parts of the cranium and the two first cervical vertebrae.

The Monster faced Eastward, his name, according to some natives who accompanied us, was Inkitchetch, and the monuments at the sides corresponded to the two sons of the present Ankou (chief), who so informed us himself on our return from this excursion. Even more notable was another deposit no more than two musket shots from that already described, and although its object was the same, to shelter one casket and elevate another to a greater distance from the ground, its paintings and adornments, their hair which from the ends of the poles which served to support the chamber and on one high posterior peak, put there probably to remind the passer-by of the person whose ashes were deposited there, all gave to the place an admirable prominence which was enhanced by the beauty of the surroundings. Some officers of the *Descubierta* who visited this place in company of the Ankau, were able to ascertain that it was the sepulchre of one of his wives. D. Antonio Tova found a similar group of monuments on Pineda Island, facing the same direction and with the same monster, which leads us to believe that each family sets up its own particular monument which, made of wood and afterwards neglected, in a few years falls victim to the weather."

Alexander Mackenzie reported no detached totem poles among the Bella Coola whom he visited in 1793. But he did describe interior house posts which are common through the totempolar region and more widely used than any other carved pole or post on the Northwest Coast.

In describing a native house, Mackenzie says in part, "The ground-plot of it was fifty feet by forty-five; each end is formed by four stout posts, fixed perpendicularly in the ground. The corner ones are plain, and support a beam of the whole length, having three intermediate props on each side, but of a larger size, and eight or nine feet in height. The two centre posts, at each end, are two feet and a half in diameter, and carved into human figures, supporting two ridge poles on their heads, at

twelve feet from the ground. The figures at the upper part of this square represent two persons with their hands upon their knees, as if they supported the weight with pain and difficulty; the others opposite to them stand at their ease, with their hands resting on their hips. In the area of the building there were the remains of several fires. The posts, poles, and figures were painted red and black; but the sculpture of these people is superior to their painting."

Captain George Vancouver who visited the Northwest Coast in 1793-94 described various mortuary poles that he saw. Near Cape Spencer he wrote, "Here were erected two pillars sixteen feet high, and four feet in circumference, painted white; on the top of each was placed a large square box; on examining one of them it was found to contain many ashes and pieces of burnt bones, which were considered to be human; these relics were carefully wrapped up in skins and old mats, and at the base of the pillars was placed an old canoe in which were some paddles."

Near Point Adolphus, Vancouver continues, "a box was found about four feet square, placed upon

SUKKWAN VILLAGE. This early view is important in that it shows the "Old Witch" totem pole in its original setting. Sukkwan, Howkan and Klinkwan were abandoned gradually when the "Citizen's Town" of Hydaburg was laid out in 1912 across the channel from Sukkwan.

THE RANCHE, SITKA'S INDIAN VILLAGE. The *Ranche*, as it was called in early Russian days, was the Indian section of Sitka. All of these houses were of Indian architecture—a single room with a bonfire in the center. This picture is believed to have been taken in 1878. The houses were destroyed two or three years later in a Navy-ordered slum clearance program. Large frame buildings soon took their place and the area is still the Indian Village.

wooden pillars about six feet from the ground. This box contained the remains of a human body very carefully wrapped up, and by its side was erected a pole about twenty feet high, painted in horizontal streaks red and white; the colors fresh and lively and from the general neatness of the whole, it was supposed to be the sepulchre of some chief.

A year earlier, June 1793, at 52 degrees 17 minutes north, on the mainland, Vancouver saw decorated houses and detached totem poles which might not have been mortuaries, in which case they would be the earliest reported detached totem poles other than mortuary. Vancouver's brief description is as follows, "The gable ends were decorated with curious painting, and near one or two of the most conspicuous mansions were carved figures in large logs of timber, representing a gigantic human form, with strange and uncommonly distorted features."

Although Maurelle apparently saw no totem poles at Sitka in 1775, thirty years later Captain Urey Lisiansky, who arrived at that place in August 1805 on the *Neva*, saw a great many mortuary poles. He wrote: "The bodies here are burned, and the ashes, together with the bones that remain unconsumed, deposited in wooden boxes which are placed on pillars that have different figures painted and carved on them, according to the wealth of the deceased.

On taking possession of our new settlement we destroyed a hundred at least of these, and I examined many of the boxes."

Lisiansky agreed with Marchand that the colors were black, light green and dark red. A predecessor of the Haida house pole which they later borrowed, was just appearing, for Lisiansky wrote: "These families however, always live apart; and, to distinguish the caste to which they belong, they place on the top of their houses, carved in wood or painted, the bird or beast that represents it."

Captain Otto von Kotzebue who was in Sitka in 1825, only twenty years after Lisiansky, apparently saw no totem poles of the mortuary type for he wrote, "The dead are burned, and their ashes preserved in small wooden boxes, in buildings appropriated to that purpose. They have a confused notion of immortality, and this is the only trace of religion which appears amongst them. They have neither priests, idols, nor any description of worship, but they place great faith in witchcraft, and the sorcerers, who are also their physicians, are held in high estimation, though more feared than loved. . . ." As many others had done before him and since his time, Kotzebue might well have mistaken grave totems for idols had he seen any.

Captain Sir Edward Belcher briefly described Sitka which he visited in 1837 but he, too, makes no mention of totem poles. Yet, on page 104 of his account, he has a sketch of a native tomb, raised slightly off the ground and decorated with totemic designs. Behind it rises a pillar on which there is an *orb* surmounted by a cross. This symbol of kingly power and justice no doubt was introduced by Europeans as it is foreign to any design found in Northwest Coast decorative art.

Jonathan Green, a missionary who toured the Northwest Coast in 1829 with the idea of establishing a mission saw totem poles, probably at Kaigani. He writes in part, "They occasionally build a decent house, and erect before it a mast or log of wood of great size carved and painted fantastically . . ." Green was from Hawaii, but apparently he saw no connection between Polynesian and Northwest Coast art and craft.

Sir George Simpson visited both Canadian and Alaskan villages and Hudson's Bay posts in 1841-42 but makes no mention of totem poles encountered except for mortuaries at Sitka. He did, however, pay tribute to the native artists when he wrote, "they carve steamers, animals, etc. very neatly in stone, wood, and ivory, imitating, in short, everything that they see, either in reality or in drawings. . . ."

In describing native mortuary customs at Sitka, Simpson wrote: "Lastly, the ashes were collected into an ornamental box, which was ultimately to be elevated on a scaffold, or on the top of a pole. On the side of a neighboring hill we saw a vast number of these monuments, which presented a very curious appearance."

The foregoing accounts cover a period of exploration of one hundred years duration and contain about all that has been recorded concerning totem poles in that century. From them we may infer that interior house posts were in general use throughout the entire region before the coming of white men; that the mortuary pole was common in Tlingit and Haida villages; that the exterior house post is Haida in origin, probably originating on Langara Island. Also that the detached totem pole must be of fairly recent origin, possibly not over a hundred and fifty years old; that totem poles in general reached their highest development during the period of white trade and occupation, roughly between 1840 and 1880.

There are two good reasons why the detached totem pole developed since the advent of Europeans. First, white men brought in great quantities of iron which made woodcarving a simple and speedy process thereby substantially reducing the cost and time involved; second, the trade in sea otter pelts had brought unheard-of wealth to the various chiefs and their clans. With this new affluence, the chiefs sought to raise their relative social statuses by giving great *potlatches* and other ceremonials at which time they took on new names and honors. Having no system of writing, they originated

WRANGELL TOTEMS. In this early view one will notice how crude these poles are when compared to Haida poles of even date. Wealthier families were able to employ professional Haida carvers but these happen to be home-made. The community house at the left boasts a front of commercial siding, windows and a door, but the rest is Indian, including the smoke hole on the roof.

Winter & Pond.

ALERT BAY, B.C. This view of Alert Bay taken 40 years ago demonstrates that the Kwakiutl Indians were carving and erecting totem poles long after the Tlingit, Haida and Tsimshian had abandoned the practice.

The Thunderbird totem poles in the foreground are the most popular on the entire Northwest Coast. Figures from top to bottom are Thunderbird, Grisly Bear, Slave, and Chief's Copper. (See story)

the detached totem pole and erected it to serve as a witness to and a validation of these important steps up the social ladder. In a word, these monuments in cedar were public documents.

The rivalry between clans became so intense that bitter feuds arose over the length and quality of these poles. Barbeau records an instance wherein one chief raised a totem pole all out of proportion to his social status and was forced by a more powerful rival to cut it down to his size, that is, his relative importance to his neighbors. Others were made to remove crests to which they had no ancestral right or to which some other clan held priority rights. Chiefs, new rich, but without inherited heraldic symbols, took new ones derived from white contacts, such as the bull, picket fence, ship or saint. Claiming to have been the first to see such wonders gave them the right. The Sitka newspaper, "The Alaskan" of Feb. 9, 1901 had a story telling of a group of the clan *Kiksadi* who were arrested for chopping down a frog emblem that had been erected

by the *Kluk-na-ha-dee* clan at a potlatch some three years earlier. The Kiksadis whose own principal emblem is the frog believed that the Kluk-na-ha-dee had no right to it but the law, white man's, that is, saw otherwise and Skoo-e-is, Koo-kwat, Ko-klu-klit, and Too-yet were sentenced to three months in jail for their offense.

The *Golden Age* of the totempole was the period of some forty or fifty years that ended about 1880. Strangely, this is the most poorly documented period in the history of the totem pole since the discovery of the Northwest Coast. Yet in those few years when the Indians were relatively unmolested and left to their own devices the whole Coast suddenly blossomed in elaborate totemic columns and gaily-decorated community houses the likes of which had never been seen before, and then, just as abruptly, faded away. There was a brief revival around 1900 occasioned by the discovery of gold near Juneau in 1880 and the Klondike stampede in 1897-98. At that time money accumulated from wages or packing on the Chilcoot trail paid for a brief revival of potlatching and house building and even some poles were erected but the cultural revival was shortlived and inferior to that of earlier times.

James Deans, a Scotsman who came to this region as an employee of the Hudson's Bay Company in 1853 is perhaps the best authority on what brought this about. In his little book, "Tales from the Totems of the Hidery" he tells the story in few words and in convincing style. For that reason, I quote him directly: "About 1832, a number of whaling ships used to winter, while on the North Pacific, at Skidegate. These whalers came chiefly from Boston or Maine. On one of these ships was a certain Captain Jefferson, who for some reason made up his mind to leave the sea and stay on shore amongst the Hidery. He seems to have had considerable means. On shore he made his home with a family, where he lived a number of years, and died in the latter thirties at the Indian's house, leaving all his money and effects to his host. According to the social laws of the Hidery, when anyone died, leaving his or her prop-erty to another, the one who inherited it had also to take the name of the donor. So this family took the name of Jefferson by which they have been known ever since. Having thus acquired so much additional property, they became the wealthiest family in the village, excepting the chief. This induced him to build a new house with totem pole, showing higher social standing in the tribe. In order to find something to carve on his pole, he adopted a part of the coat-of-arms of the chief, which he thought he had a right to, his wife being the chief's sister. As soon as the chief knew Jefferson's intentions, he told him that on no account would he allow his crest to be quartered. Jefferson knew it would not do to oppose the chief, so he said: "Skidegat won't allow me to take part of his crest, so I will have one of my own made and show him who is richest and at the same time leave no bare space like the poorer people." So when his pole was set up, it had three rows of the *tau* or copper cross money, one in front and one on each side, in addition to his family crests. When the chief died, Jefferson took down his

TOTEMS OF TUXEKAN. If one were to go to the site of old Tuxekan today he would see nothing but the forest. Yet the dead are there even though their memorials have moldered away. All the poles in this area that could be saved or duplicated may be seen today in the Klawock Totem Park.

W. H. Case photo.

ALERT BAY TOTEM. To visitors, the most popular totem poles on the Coast were those of the Kwakiutl Indians who live near the Northern tip of Vancouver Island and adjoining country. Here is Thunderbird perched on the head of Grisly Bear, guardian of his property. (See story.) Photo by Merle LaVoy.

imitation copper money pole, and in its place put up another with the late chief's coat-of-arms quartered, including the story connected with it.

As I said before, none but chiefs were able to put up elaborately carved columns, with ancient stories on them, up to the years 1830 or later. From that date on to 1880 the Hidery began to go abroad as sailors and otherwise mix with the white settlers, where by labor and other means they acquired money and goods. These were sent home to their relations, in order to help them to have fine houses and totem poles. For that purpose every means was used. Soon the common people became richer than the chiefs and had better houses and more elaborate totem poles. Soon an active competition commenced, each one trying to have the best. Wives, sisters and mothers would prostitute themselves, in order to obtain the wherewithal to get ahead of the others. Some died in the mad race for wealth and today the unfinished houses stand a beautiful ruin, sad mementos of the past.

While some were busy with this building and carving, others were busy collecting all the old stories to be found, bearing on their respective crests, from the old folks and from the ancient mythology of the Hidery. By these means many an old legend and myth, all but forgotten, was revived; even distant tribes were applied to and many an ancient tale, still lingering in the memories of the old folks, was brought to light. These tales, as soon as found, were carved on the totem poles of the parties, who by the social laws of the Hidery were entitled to them. By these means many an old story was preserved."

A number of things conspired to end the totem-pole's Golden Age as abruptly as it had begun. Among them were smallpox, the abolition of slavery, the coming of salteries and salmon canneries, and the white man's shack and the airtight heater. Contributing also were Canadian law which forbade the Potlatch, missionary influence, and the generally cheapening of an institution which was once the exclusive right of the nobles. Like the *tinneh* or chief's copper which became virtually meaningless when mass-produced, so now the true heraldic pole was cheapened by the gaudy monuments of the new rich. The old aristocracy was falling apart and with it went its symbols.

Smallpox so decimated the Haida nation that out of a population of nine or ten thousand, only about six hundred were left in the Queen Charlotte Islands and about the same number in Alaska. Whole Tlingit villages were wiped out. Others, stricken by the dread disease, were abandoned forever as cursed. Many natives flocked to the vicinity of salteries, canneries and gold mines. There they were crowded into small, ill-made, poorly ventilated shacks where tuberculosis took up where smallpox left off. Those who remained in the tribal villages had to abandon the huge community houses, for without slave labor they could not be heated or otherwise maintained. The airtight heater was the solution but it called for smaller houses, for fuel, although abundant on the stump, was a serious problem in wintertime. The airtight heater with its low fuel consumption, made it possible for the menfolks to prepare enough fuel in advance that they could go trapping in winter, or hunting and fishing at great distances from home, leaving their families behind for the first time. Freed from their primitive daily chores, the Indian men were becoming wage earners and their households began to differ but little from those of the earlier pioneers now filtering into the region. Where once they were seasonally nomadic gatherers, more settled life now opened the way for the establishing of missions and schools among them. Towns, rather than winter villages were coming into being, and in them totem poles were considerably out of harmony and useless.

A few desultory attempts at totem pole carving has continued until the present day, particularly between 1880 and 1900 as may be judged from newspaper accounts of that time. Newspapers at last were beginning to record what was happening to the Indians in their struggle for readjustment to a culture that had been forced upon them and had inadvertently destroyed their own.

A traveler on the mailboat *Iris* quoted in the Sitka *Alaskan* Jan. 15, 1887 gives a hint of what happened when the first salmon cannery in Alaska was established at Klawock in 1879 and the natives from the surrounding villages flocked there for the employment offered. He wrote: "Leaving Klawock we returned by the way of *Tuksekan*, a village of the *Hanegahs*. It is becoming quite dilapidated and is not much used except as a winter home. It has the largest display of totem sticks of any village I have visited . . ."

The same newspaper under date of July 23, 1887 has this from its Wrangell correspondent: "An Indian named Kadashan is having built a two-storey residence on the site of his old house, with two sets of bay windows above and below. The building is a frame one covered with rustic with building paper under it. It will be finished inside with lumber and looks as if it will be one of the nicest in the country. Beat that if you can."

This was the new home of Chief Kadashan whose totem poles stood on Wrangell's main street where they had been placed after removal from their original site on the beach near the sawmill. When they rotted beyond repair duplicates were made and placed in a cluster on Shakes Island for the benefit of tourists.

In the Alaskan of May 12, 1888 was this item: The *Elder* brought from Metlakatla two old totem poles consigned to Dr. Sheldon Jackson, for the Sitka Museum. It seems that formerly the people now living at Port Tongass resided at Port Chester. Fifty years ago a party of Stickeens attacked and defeated them. The village was burned and the people driven away. The totem poles alone seemed to have escaped the fire. Last summer, when the Metlakahtlans took possession of the place, they found a few still standing. Having no interest in them, the poles were gradually being destroyed. The best two remaining were secured for the Museum.

The Kake natives, always jealous of their tribal institutions, were still carving memorial poles as late as 1895. An item appearing in the *Alaska Searchlight* of Juneau on Dec. 21, 1895 stated: "The *Mayflower* returned from Kake Tuesday night. The Kake Indians erected a large and elaborately carved totem last Monday in honor of a dead chief and were indulging in the usual potlatch. A large number of natives were present but everyone seemed disposed to be peaceable."

On February 29, 1896 the Alaskan published an extract from a letter written by Dr. Thwing of Wrangell as follows: "This winter there has been a

KWAKIUTL TOTEM. Photographed at Alert Bay some 30 years ago, this gaily painted bird is a classical example of Kwakiutl Indian art. If it was meant to depict Thunderbird it has since lost its ear-like plumes.

Photo by author.

TUXEKAN CLUSTER. Like the Kake totem poles, most of the others between there and Klawock were short memorials with squared shafts. Replicas of many of these may now be seen in the Klawock Totem Park.

very general feeling of suspense and expectancy in view of the great feast and intertribal dance for which Chief Shakes has been preparing for a year or two. To dignify a living son, and commemorate one dead, there has been a new totem pole carved, and the Tongass natives have been called to dance and feast here. These guests arrived February 1st, and were received with great honor and much noise."

This was the *Raven* pole still standing in Wrangell and in fair condition despite its roundly seventy years. However, it has been repaired and repainted from time to time by Wrangell citizens, which has contributed immeasurably to its preservation.

The so-called *Kiksadi* pole, one of the most popular in Alaska, was set up in Wrangell in the fall of 1895 in front of the *Sun House*. In the record of the probate proceedings in the estate of *Caltine* (Kolteen), his widow waived her rights to the house "in consideration of certain debts having been assumed by Willis Hoagland, the lineal chieftain, and the further consideration of having a totem erected to the honor of my husband and his gens. . . ." This agreement was signed February 11, 1895 and the memorial pole was raised later that year.

The *Mining Journal* of Ketchikan, issue of Jan.

18, 1902 gives evidence that totem poles were being carved there after the turn of the century although it is difficult to determine just which poles they are referring to. The item is as follows: "The natives have about completed a new totem pole, which they intend erecting at the foot of Main Street as soon as the finishing touches can be applied. Another of the same pattern is being built in Indian town." Chief Johnson's pole was carved at about that time but there is no record of another of the same pattern having been carved.

Totem pole carving reached the natives of the upper Skeena River much later than it did the coastal Tsimshian, Haida and Southern Tlingit and was consequently carried on longer, in fact, until quite recently. The Kwakiutl and Nootka Indians also got a late start, none of the fine cluster at Alert Bay having been carved prior to 1890. There several were erected during the 1930's. But in nearly all cases, if not all, the original function of the various monuments in cedar has been discontinued and no totem poles are carved except for sale or in rehabilitation programs conducted by various agencies both in British Columbia and in Alaska. One of this nature was erected in Juneau in 1963.

SON-I-YAT'S CANOE. On Oct. 31, 1901 the revenue cutter *Rush* steamed into Sitka harbor with a gift to the District of Alaska from Haida Chief Son-i-yat of Kasaan. The present consisted of a tall totem pole that had stood before the chief's Community House, and the four house pillars from within it. These were restored, repainted, and set up in Sitka's Totem Park near the mouth of Indian River. Included also was this large war canoe, 47 feet long and six feet wide, bearing at its bow the Killerwhale emblem with the Raven emblem near the stern. For many years this canoe was to be seen displayed in the open area in front of the Pioneers Home. Children played in it and eventually dry rot took its toll. When it began to fall apart, passersby helped themselves to cedar fragments for kindling wood. And eventually it existed only in the memory of the town's oldest residents.

E. L. Merrill Photo.

KAKE VILLAGE IN 1905. Kake never did have many totem poles and what it did have were small. Only a half dozen are to be seen in this view, behind the houses where mortuary poles are usually found. The church is that of the Society of Friends, that is, Quakers. But it was when the Presbyterians took over the mission that the totem poles were mysteriously dynamited and burned. (See text.)

HAIDA VILLAGE OF HOWKAN. Taken more than 80 years ago, this rare view of Howkan near Alaska's southern border shows a typical elaborate heraldic totem pole. The pole is surmounted by the totem Eagle beneath which sits the *watchman*. Then follows a heraldic myth, now long forgotten and perhaps beyond recognition by anyone living today.

Davidson Photo.

THE KYAN TOTEM POLE. This early photograph depicts Chief Kyan's totem pole still to be seen in downtown Ketchikan. The top figure is Crane, middle figure is Thunderbird, and the lower one is the Grisly Bear.

Chapter Four

TYPES OF TOTEM POLES

What is generally referred to as a totem pole may be any one of a half dozen or more types of cedar monuments found on the Northwest Coast that have been variously described by travellers as totem poles, totem posts, totem pillars, house posts and totem sticks. The one thing that they have in common is that they were all carved of red cedar in the traditional Northwest Coast art style and none of those extant could really be considered ancient because of the perishable nature of wood in a wet country. Their differences from each other lay in their use and the purpose for which they were erected. However, there was one thing the exterior monuments had in common: they were all set up to validate some important act or event hence were *public documents* of a people who as yet had not invented a system of writing or borrowed one from someone else.

The six types of these sculptured cedar monuments in the order of their probable development are: the house pillar and false house pillar, mortuary pole, memorial pole, heraldic portal pole, potlatch pole, and ridicule or shame pole.

The house pillar was in common use throughout the entire totempolar region by the time of the earliest explorations which is more than can be said of any of the other types. The Haidas used four of these pillars to support the central rafters of their massive community houses. Their carvings illustrated stories from Haida mythology and sometimes one story was so long and well illustrated that it was continued from pole to pole, occupying all four. Tribes to the south imitated the Haida pillar but it became less ornate the farther it was removed from Haida influence.

The Tlingit did not usually carve the posts on which the house beams actually rested but placed a decorative false pillar against plain supporting pillars so that the effect was the same as in the Haida house. This might have been due to the fact that in most of the Tlingit territory there was no red cedar or it was too small to supply the broad decorative pillars so much admired by these people. Consequently, after the house was built of local materials, imported false pillars made by professional artisans from Wrangell or localities south of there would be installed. An advantage of this practice was that these costly pillars could be removed at some later date and installed in a new house and this was actually done at Wrangell.

Apparently some houses had eight decorative pillars, for Swanton in the 26th Annual Report of the Bureau of American Ethnology states, "when he was about to undertake any task a man who had eight house posts in his house had to fast eight days, one for each post. Slaves were always

51

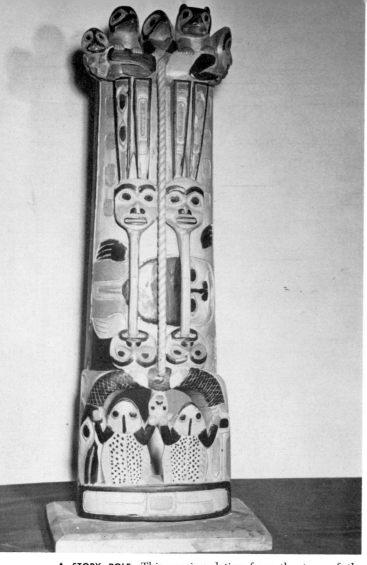

A STORY POLE. This carving dating from the turn of the century could be termed a story book, since one can recognize references to several different stories on it. The two central figures with long necks are the heads of the giant kelp down which Raven crawled to get a sea urchin when he was endeavoring to persuade *Tide Woman* to release the tides. Bear tracks are seen leading to the bear on top who lead the Indians to safety during a flood. Also seen on top is *Octopus,* a figure in several stories, and *Kooshtakah,* the bogey man. Some halibut-like creatures are seen at the bottom beneath an arch formed by a reptilian sea creature.

killed and their bodies thrown into the holes in which the house posts were to be stood."

The above-mentioned custom of dispatching slaves and placing their bodies in the holes in which totem poles were to be erected is doubtless very old and long-since abandoned although stories of it still persist in all of the native villages. It was significant that no bones were found beneath any of the poles removed from their original positions during the

U.S. Forest Service restoration program in the late 1930's. In a number of instances native workmen employed in removing the poles predicted that skeletons would be found beneath certain poles and were amazed when none were found there. Evidence that the custom was abandoned many years ago is seen in a pair of restored house pillars now in the State Museum in Juneau. The motif of the pillars is the sea lion but also carved thereon is a broad red ring surrounding a human face. The rim represents the post hole dug by the slave who remained in it and who, at his master's command to open his mouth, received the pillar which thereafter rested on his body. It is said by Tlingit informants that the carving was resorted to after it became necessary to abandon the cruel and inhumane practice.

Due to the fact that house pillars were indoors and moved to new houses periodically they are the oldest examples of sculpture to be seen in the native villages today. At Klukwan, seat of the Chilkats, no less than four houses still retain their house pillars although the houses themselves are now of modern construction. In the *Whale House* are four handsome posts still retaining their native paint. Sitka also has house posts in several of the houses in the native section although this fact was not generally known, even to resident Sitkans until recently. Lately on *Alaska Day* several Sitka community houses are opened to the public by their owners at which time these and other treasures may be viewed.

These pillars are often beautifully inlaid with bluegreen abalone shell, and in some cases decorated with human hair and ermine. At Wrangell, in the reconstructed Chief Shakes community house are four houseposts from an earlier house at Old Wrangell or *Kotslitan.* It was once considered a chiefly act to chop a figure from one of these priceless pillars, and one of the Wrangell pillars has been thus defaced. To these people, a post thus disfigured increased in value and the owner gained importance among his associates for his vandalism.

Louis Shotridge, a Chilkat Indian ethnologist, writing in the Museum Journal of the University of Pennsylvania (1913) has this to say about house pillars: "With the introduction of steel and iron implements among the tribes of the Northwest Coast, totem poles became numerous. Numbers of them could be seen in front of houses in the more southern villages. But before the modern tools, it is said,

SON-I-YAT OR "GOV. BRADY" TOTEM POLE. This totem pole, restored, together with the four house pillars, was the gift of Son-i-yat, Haida Chief of Kasaan, to the District of Alaska through Gov. Brady. It was brought to Sitka in 1902 by the Revenue Cutter *Rush* and erected by prisoners. It is regarded as Alaska's finest totem pole.
Photo by courtesy of the Photo Shop Studio, Sitka.

THE GONAKADET AND THE SUPERNATURAL GRIZZLY BEAR. These are the original mortuaries that stood before Shakes' house in Wrangell. Duplicates now stand in the exact spot. The Gonakadet pole on the left held the ashes of Chief Shakes VI's father and mother. The ashes of his younger brother were deposited in the grizzly bear pole to the right. (See Stories of these poles.)

(Photo by author).

totem poles were rare, not only on account of the difficulty in the making—as stone and wood were used for tools—but the desire to keep them strictly distinctive was a reason for their scarcity.

"One often hears it said by the older people that originally totem poles were used inside of the houses only, to support the roof beams. The carvings and paintings on them were usually those of the family crests. These posts were regarded with respect very much as the flag of a nation. Even when the Chilkats had acquired modern tools with which to make totem poles they did not fill their villages with tall poles like some other tribes, chiefly because they wanted to keep to the original idea.

"The figures seen on a totem pole are the principal subjects taken from tradition treating of the family's history. These traditions may treat of the family's rise to prominence or of the heroic exploit of one of its members. From such subjects the crests are derived. . . ."

Another reason why the Chilkats did not go in for tall totem poles is that they are several hundred miles beyond the range of the giant red cedars required for their manufacture. The best of these grow in the Queen Charlotte Islands and none of any consequence exist north of Wrangell. Even for their interior house posts the Chilkats had to import cedar logs and artisans from Wrangell or, still more likely, the finished pillars that had been made to order in Wrangell or some other place where the big cedars grew.

The mortuary pole as first observed by explorers in the Tlingit country where this pole is most common, consisted simply of a plain, sometimes painted, pole on top of which a box containing ashes of the dead were placed. Later, a totem figure was placed at the top and the ashes deposited in a crypt excavated at the back of the pole. This type is the most common totem pole found in Alaska. A later development was to further embellish the monument by having a story carved thereon, as in heraldic or potlatch poles. The Kadashan poles at Wrangell are a good example of this type. The mortuary pole went out as the missionaries came in for they introduced the Christian burial and in very few years cremation ceased except in isolated instances.

Memorial poles had a variety of functions. In Tlingit territory they doubled for the Haida potlatch poles and upon the passing of the mortuary pole they were erected much in the manner of tomb stones although generally at a distance from the grave. They were not necessarily raised for the dead alone, but could honor the living, as well. The Raven pole at Wrangell was erected by Chief Shakes VI in honor of a dead and a living son.

Memorial poles were erected by the nephew or brother of a dead chief within a year of his taking his deceased uncle or brother's place, this being part of his obligation.

The heraldic or family pole was first observed on Langara Island, Queen Charlotte Islands in 1790 as mentioned earlier. It was placed against the middle front of the house and a hole near its base served as the doorway to the house. It was originally short and broad but as years went on and rivalries increased, evolved into a tall, stately monument, beautifully carved and painted. Its legend was from the mythological history of the family residing within and was designed to advertize and exalt the lineage of those who dwelt within. This type of pole spread to the neighboring Tsimshian, Tlingit, Bella Bella and Kwakiutl.

The potlatch pole of the Haidas as we know it, is a most recent development of the totem pole family, probably not over a hundred and fifty years old at the most. It was the result of the accumulation of wealth in the hands of middle class Indians, resulting from the fur trade, wages sent home by Indian seamen and the gains of women from prostitution at Victoria, plus good steel tools. New-rich chiefs now began to vie with one another, socially, and each sought to raise their respective social standings through means of the potlatch. The poles erected to record and validate such events were detached, elaborately carved, and painted, and of great height, some reaching from sixty to eighty feet. Beginning about 1850 and continuing until 1880, Haida, Tsimshian, and Tlingit sought to outdo each other in erecting these handsome monuments. Where once they were the exclusive emblem of the

SHAKES' HOUSE AND MORTUARIES. When one chief faced his dwelling with lumber and set in windows and a door, they all followed suit. Beyond that, the house remained the same until stoves took the place of the open fire. These mortuary poles once held the ashes of Shakes's relatives but they have since been replaced with duplicates, sans ashes.

A RIDICULE POLE. The totem of the Three Frogs stands on Shakes' Island where an earlier "original" stood a hundred years ago. According to a generally accepted version, three Kiksadi women married three of Shakes' slaves and lived with them in the Shakes household. After a time Shakes demanded pay from the Kiksadi chief for the keep of these women. The Kiksadis, on the other hand, refused to have anything to do with the women, holding they were not responsible for them since they had lowered themselves by marrying slaves. After requesting payment three times, Shakes ordered the three women carved in the form of the Kiksadi emblem, the frog, and placed on a rack where they were to remain the objects of public ridicule until the debt was paid. The Kiksadi, having disowned the women, never paid the debt so the original pole remained until it rotted away.

(Photo by the author).

old and distinguished nobility, now they were paraded everywhere by the newly rich. The fad went one hundred and fifty miles inland, up the Skeena river, where it continued until after 1900. The Kwakiutl at Alert Bay didn't get started until after 1890 but were still erecting them there less than a generation ago.

The potlatch pole of the Haidas is called *se-at-lang-lae-ee*, that is, *story-master*, which it actually is, or *wath-lal* which is their word for potlatch. It means, *give-more*, which is what you are expected to do in return after receiving a *potlatch*, meaning a gift with a string attached. This will be discussed later since we are concerned only with the pole at the moment. This monument can often be distinguished by its having at the top, from one to three highhatted *watchmen*. Only the wealthiest chiefs could afford three. Beneath the watchmen is the totem of the chief who gave the Potlatch and had the pole carved and erected. Then follows a myth belonging to the chief and finally, near the base, the totem of his wife. It is only on a pole of this type

that the opposite totems of a man and his wife appear. In this case it is necessary in order to show that she also has an interest in the proceeds to come from the Potlatch represented by this pole. The great number of toads seen protruding from ears, eyes and in vacant spaces are said by some to have been carved there "to prevent the pole from rotting." Actually their function was merely that of space-fillers.

The sixth type of totem pole is called the *ridicule* or *shame* pole. It is most often erected for the purpose of forcing some person of high standing to meet or recognize an obligation. Possibly more of these were erected to shame white men than native chiefs for often when a white man appears on a totem pole it is to hold him up to public scorn. It is said that the Haidas sometimes carved a person on a pole upside down for the same purpose. However, a commoner Haida practice when a man failed to pay his debts was to *put him on a blanket*. In this instance the party to whom the debt was owed would have a blanket made, on which the totem of the debtor appeared. Whenever the creditor wore this the debtor was shamed. His only recourse was to *buy the blanket,* this is, pay the debt and destroy the blanket.

Perhaps the best example of a Tlingit ridicule pole extant is the one based on an old drawing that was reconstructed at Wrangell on Chief Shakes' Island. It consists of a T-shaped roost on which are perched three huge frogs. These are said to represent three Kiksadi women (whose clan symbol is the frog) allegedly guilty of consorting with three of Chief Shakes' slaves. After a time Shakes presented the Kiksadi chief with a bill for their keep since the women were living in his household. However, the Kiksadi chief refused to pay, holding that the women had disgraced themselves by their actions and had been ejected from the clan, hence he was no longer responsible for their keep. Shakes thought otherwise so, according to custom, he sought to force payment through the ridicule pole method. Whether or not the debt was ever recognized and paid is unknown today. But when the pole was duplicated word got around and considerable feeling was aroused among the Kiksadi descendants still living there. Some believed that the debt had been paid, others felt that time had erased the debt if it still existed. Threats were made to destroy it before it could be set up. But eventually calmer judgment prevailed and the pole was erected so the restoration could be complete. It has never been molested.

It is said that at Sitka a ridicule pole was once erected to shame a white trader who had been adopted into the Raven phratry with considerable ceremony and had been given presents. According to custom he should have reciprocated by giving a potlatch in due time at which time he would repay his benefactor with interest. Failing in this, the disgruntled chief had the ridicule pole carved and erected. It showed the white man at the top in the form of a raven, while in a series of holes running the length of the pole, appeared the robber woodpecker angrily protesting that the white man had usurped his place by becoming a bigger thief than he was.

Kake village is also said to have had a ridicule pole which was erected to show contempt for a Russian that had killed one of the tribesmen. The Russian was carved realistically at the top of the pole and beneath it was a raven attacking a halibut. The halibut, being white, represents the white man and the two figures convey the idea that the murder would be avenged.

Memorial and mortuary poles have their modern versions which may be seen in any cemetery in Southeastern Alaska and coastal British Columbia. These are marble and granite tombstones on which the totems or clan symbols of the dead are carved to order at commercial monumental works. But the ridicule idea also has found its way into modern cemeteries. A few years ago a prominent Kake native received the disquieting news that his mother, long since dead, was being ridiculed on a tombstone on Shustak's Point in Wrangell. He and his clan were greatly distressed and at the end of the prosperous fishing season, pooled their profits and went to Wrangell to investigate the rumor. What took place there is not known to the writer but the group returned some days later bearing a marble tombstone on which had been carved the likeness of a woman. Several days later a large public gathering took place in the home of the fisherman at the con-

KATALLA HOUSE PILLARS. These pillars were taken from a Tlingit Community House between Katalla and Yakataga Beach. No totem poles are recorded from any point north of Katalla, the high-water mark of Tlingit northern expansion. Pioneer Dr. Will Chase of Cordova is seen standing between the pillars which subsequently were lost in a fire which destroyed his office and invaluable collection of early Alaskana.

(Photo courtesy Dr. Will Chase).

MODEL POTLATCH POLE. It is not known to the author if a full-sized pole like this was ever erected but it tells of a potlatch given by a group that frowned on exterior totem poles, the Chilkat *Ganaxadi,* a Raven clan that displayed the frog as its principal clan symbol.

At the top is the Phratry symbol, Raven, of the Chief who presumably gave the potlatch, and with it the frog (actually a toad). At the bottom is the Wolf Phratry symbol (equates with Raven), and the Clan symbol, *Grisly Bear,* representing the chief's wife. In between a story is told, by way of decoration, of the cannibal giant, *Gooteekhl.* He is shown holding half a frog in his hands, the half-frog representing the decimated Ganaxadi clan in his power. Beneath is *Mosquito* stabbing frog. This recalls the threat that the cannibal made to the Indians who cremated him alive, that "even though you burn me, I'll still eat your people!" Hot sparks from his pyre turned into myriads of mosquitos that still "eat the people." (See story)

clusion of which the group re-assembled beside the house where the offending tombstone was publicly knocked to pieces with a sledge hammer. Thus a long-time debt, real or fancied, was paid and the evidence of it publicly destroyed. In this case it appears that the creditors had kept the debt a secret until they felt the debtor was financially able to make a substantial settlement.

There may have been other posts set up as witnesses for various transactions but they were not likely to be of long duration or ornate enough to be confused with totems. One of these types would be the posts set up during the buying and selling of a chief's copper. During the period when their value was computed in two dollar Hudson's Bay blankets it was necessary that the public be informed as to the number of blankets paid for a certain copper since the value of the copper went up with each sale. So when the price was finally agreed upon, a post was set up and the blankets stacked against it to the top then continued down the beach until the end of the stack was reached. There a similar post was set up. After the blankets were removed these posts remained to remind the public of the size of the stack. And since some of these named coppers brought as much as nine thousand blankets, the distance between the posts must have been considerable. Mention perhaps should be made of the miniature totem poles or story masters that the Haida carvers started making sometime after 1820 when a black indurated clay or shale stone was discovered on the Queen Charlotte Islands near the head of Skidegate Inlet. About that time the sea otter became so depleted that the Haidas had to find something else to trade and their so-called slate carvings caught on. At first they copied things seen on the trading ships or made art objects to order such as trays, pipes, plaques etc. in an alien style. But they soon abandoned this type of carving and began to employ their own art style, eventually concentrating on model totem poles. Since many more of these were made of stone than of wood, it is quite likely that the later carvers of tall cedar poles used them for models. Certainly the style is the same in the Haida poles.

A few of the argillite poles are still being made but the old masters like Charlie Edensaw of Masset are gone and no new craftsmen have appeared to take their places. For those who would like to pursue the study of argillite carving and carvers further, Dr. Marius Barbeau's book, "Haida Carvers" is an excellent reference.

THE DEVIL'S THUMB TOTEM. No longer standing on Shustak's Point, Wrangell. This pole was erected by "Flying Raven" in memory of his daughter, Wanda, who died while away at boarding school and whose mother was a "Talqoe-di." The Devil's Thumb or "Talth Qua Na Sha" is a holy mountain to the Talqoe-di for it was on it that they found refuge during the flood. The carving represents the personified mountain.

(U.S. Forest Service Photo).

HAIDA INTERIOR HOUSE PILLAR. This fine pillar standing amid the ruins of Klinkwan gives some indication of the size of the old community houses.

(Photo by author).

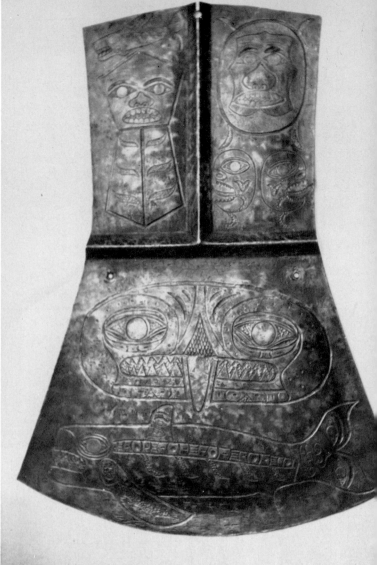

GONG-TYPE CHIEF'S COPPER. Shield-shaped copper plates were once the status symbols of the Northwest Coast. While generally believed to have been made of native copper, there is no evidence to support this belief. Actually, they were first made of commercial sheet copper brought in by Spaniards in the 18th century. The prototype was probably a greatly-enlarged version of a Tagish copper arrowhead, made on the order of some Indian chief by a ship's armorer. A few made to serve as gongs upon which slaves beat in ceremonial processions were first reported by Lisiansky at Sitka in 1805. Author's collection.

Photo by author.

THE SUN AND RAVEN POLE. Seen here in its original setting on Pennock Island opposite Ketchikan, where it was erected in 1902, this memorial pole was restored and set up in the Saxman Totem Park in 1939. Shown in the carvings are two exploits of Raven and a suggestion of a third. Above is Raven, his head encircled by the Sun whose children are shown in his lap. Raven had flown up to the Sun to escape flood waters that covered the earth. Upon his return, Raven, being curious as to what was under the sea, took a trip beneath the waves. Before going, he arranged for Frog to do his breathing for him on this journey, accounting for the presence of Frog in the carving. The central figure is believed by some to be the face of Fog Woman whose story is better told on Chief Johnson's pole. (See text.)

A GRAVE AT WRANGELL. A wolf baying at the moon is here seen above a native mortuary, influenced by Russian log construction. Before they came, the Indians always squared their timbers with adzes and made their walls of hewn planks. Opposite Old Wrangell, one of these tombs still stands, but its contents have been pilfered or moldered away. It is empty.

Chapter Five

READING A TOTEM POLE

It is a common belief that the grotesque, interlocking figures on a totem pole constitute an esoteric symbolism revealing secrets only to certain initiated tribesmen sworn never to reveal their meaning to outsiders. Some even suspected in them a primitive picture-writing akin to that of the early Mayas, Egyptians and Chinese. Much of this was due to the air of mystery that has always surrounded totem poles due to the local ignorance of both the natives and white residents, as well as the reluctance of the former to talk freely about them with strangers. As pointed out earlier, myths are property and only those who have inherited or acquired the right, have the privilege to tell a particular story. This restriction is not generally enforced today, at least in the larger towns, but in some of the native villages, sanctions would still be assessed against anyone breaking the rule.

Actually there is nothing purposely hidden in totem poles. And strangely enough, the myth carved on these monuments is only a decoration on the pole that was put up for some other purpose. These myths cannot be *read* in the strict sense of the word. Rather, it should be said that they may be *recognized,* for they contain nothing more or less than a system of memory devices which, taken in their proper sequence will recall a myth, if one already knows it, or takes the trouble to learn it. This, of course, applies only to totem poles embellished with a sculptured story, and not all of them are. Early mortuary poles often had only a single figure carved or placed at the top of a bare pole. This figure might represent the phratry symbol of the deceased or it might be his most important clan symbol. In case the chief had several, they might all appear, the most important or exclusive, in his opinion, being at the top. A person well-versed in the history of this man's clan might *read* the pole by simply reciting the stories attendant to the acquisition of each of these symbols.

Most of the stories carved on totem poles are taken from the general mythology of the tribe, principal among them being the exploits of Raven, a trickster diety. Others are of culture heroes or of progenitors, not actual, but out of the mythology. If the pole is short, such as an interior house pillar, the story might be recalled by simply carving the principal character in the act which highlights the myth. However, if the story is long and has many characters that must be introduced, it might be continued from pillar to pillar, occupying all four. In some cases a long story occupied all the space on two exterior poles that were erected simultaneously, side by side. On the other hand, if the story was short and the pole to be carved, tall, the characters might be

WASGO OR SUSAN POLE AT SITKA. This fine Haida pole stands at the entrance to Totem Lane in the Sitka National Monument. It depicts the most popular tale of mother-in-law trouble known both to the Haida and Tlingit. Here the evil woman who posed as a shaman is seen at the top. Next is the lake monster known variously as the Gonakadate, Wasgo or Susun, in a Haida form in which it has a duck-like bill. The next figure is a frog which is probably inserted as a space-filler. The young hero of the tale is shown next followed by Wasgo again in its marine form wherein it is conceived as part wolf, part killerwhale. For a full account see story.

Winter & Pond photo.

that a chief once ordered a pole carved in a certain village and then placed a duplicate order in another distant village. When the poles were completed and delivered they were placed side by side and no one could tell the one from the other.

Totem poles are read from the top downward. A Tlingit pole is often surmounted by the principal character in the legend, but not always. Sometimes the pole is topped by the phratry symbol such as Raven or Eagle, or even by a clan symbol such as Killerwhale or Grisly Bear. Some Haida potlatch poles are surmounted by from one to three high-hatted *watchmen* under which will be the symbol of the chief raising the pole. Following this will be the characters and objects figuring in the story, in sequence, and at the bottom will be the symbol of the wife's clan or phratry or both.

It may readily be seen that in order to read a totem pole, one must be well grounded in the mythology of that particular tribe. Many of these myths have been recorded and published by competent folklorists and ethnologists, and are readily obtainable in libraries. But some stories were the private property of clans and difficult to collect. Where these have been carved on totem poles long standing or now destroyed, and recorded only in old photographs and engravings it may be no longer possible to be sure what the story was.

Beyond achieving a knowledge of the oral literature of the Totempolar region, one must also acquire a fair knowledge of the art style and symbolism employed by the carvers. This is necessary in order to be able to recognize the characters appearing on the poles for what they are since the artists seldom employed realism. Many animals are shown in quasi-human form but with some devise or symbol by which they may be identified. Some also appear that have no relation to the myths, being merely space fillers. In fact, the Indian artist so abhorred undecorated spaces that he sometimes repeated a figure just to eke out the required length of the decoration.

Some knowledge of the religion of the area is required if one would understand totem poles although they are in no sense idols. For instance, these Indians believed that all animals had more or less dual personalities hence they would carve Raven sometimes as a man and sometimes as a bird, and still at other times part bird and part man. *Killerwhale* was sometimes carved with conventionalized realism but at other times the *whale* was simply the *canoe* in which *Killerwhale* rode. *Spirits* were sometimes portrayed as *eyes* and sometimes as complete faces, particularly if the space were large. The blowhole of a whale might appear as a face with

repeated or another story would begin where the first left off with nothing to indicate where the first ended and the next began.

There being many versions of each myth, it follows that no two poles decorated by the same story would be alike in all details. According to the Haidas this was not always the case at least in the Haida nation. There is an old story to the effect an open mouth, or the joints of any animal or bird as stylized *eyes*.

A study of the native religion of the Northwest Coast further reveals the belief which inspired cremation of bodies and the deposition of ashes in the backs of mortuary poles, and helps one to understand that type of pole and why it was discontinued when the Christian religion was introduced.

After one has acquired a knowledge of the local mythology, art, and religion there remains only the necessity of gaining a working knowledge of the social and political organization of the various tribes in order to read or rather, recognize totem poles. Haida poles must be recognized as such for the stories carved thereon are often different from those of the Tlingit, as are those of the Tsimshian and Kwakiutl. Even the art style differs somewhat but the differences are readily learned. A few years ago one would be certain that Tlingit poles would be found only in the territory occupied exclusively by the Tlingit Indians and Haida poles would be found

in Haida territory. However, many have been taken up and transported to new locations even within the totempolar region. Sitka, in Tlingit country, now has many fine Haida totem poles brought there from Kasaan, Howkan, and Klinkwan, and Tlingit poles brought from Port Chester on Annette Island. There is not a genuine Sitka pole in the Sitka Totem Park for only mortuary poles were originally carved there, and these have long since disappeared. A fine old Haida pole from Sukkwan stands besides the city library in Juneau and another is being erected at the dead end of Seward street as this is written. Several Haida poles from Kasaan have been transported to Ketchikan, a Tlingit town, and there are Haida poles at Totem Bight, near Ketchikan. At Prince Rupert, B.C., in Tsimshian territory there may be seen several fine Haida poles that were brought from the Queen Charlotte Islands. Wrangell's poles are all Tlingit although two show Haida style, and one was actually modeled after a Haida chief's staff. Some of the smaller poles on the main street of Wrangell are Tlingit, having been

THE KADISHAN TOTEM POLES. After initial restoration by Wrangell citizens in 1926. The pole at the left was modeled after a Haida cane presented to Chief Kadishan. When beyond further repair, these poles were duplicated and set up on Shakes Island a few blocks east.

Photo by author.

RAVEN IS CARVED ON THIS MOSS-COVERED MEMORIAL. To demonstrate his dual personality: head and wings are raven-like, body is human in form. Wrangell Cemetery.

Photo by author.

brought there from the West Coast of Prince of Wales Island.

In attempting to read a totem pole, one should first determine what linguistic group or tribe made it for this decides among which group of published myths one might find the story. Next, he must determine what type of pole it is since this is likely to affect the arrangement of figures carved thereon. With this much accomplished, he now attempts to identify each of the figures on the pole, trying to ascertain which are important and which are merely space fillers. This should be easy since space fillers are never as large as the characters, even if the character in the story is only a mouse, since the mouse would be carved as large as a mink or even larger if associated with other characters that were large. Now one has only to recall a myth of that tribe wherein all these characters and objects have a part, roughly in the sequence in which they appear on the pole, beginning with the uppermost figure.

Oftentimes, a story will be recalled that fits, but several figures will remain unaccounted for. This might be due to any one of several reasons. It might be that a fuller version of the story is carved than the one recorded, or a slightly different version. Or it might be that some of the figures are simply clan or phratry symbols used to fill out space. Again, it

is possible that more than one story has been placed on the pole. This is quite often the case if the pole is very tall, in which instance the selected story might not reach. In the event that some of the lesser characters are missing, think no more about it, for many characters and important objects are left off if the space is limited. In carving the story of *Blackface* or *Kahasi*, often only Blackface is shown in the act of rending a sealion apart. Sometimes a raven is added above to show to which phratry he belonged, and sometimes he wears a headdress of braided sealion intestines as a further recognition feature. But whatever else appears or it omitted, everyone knowing the story will recognize it if only a man is shown rending a sealion apart.

Totem poles are like the illustrations in a book. If the book is familiar to one, a well-known illustration from it will recall its name or context. But a sequence of well-chosen illustrations will recall a book only vaguely remembered. This method of arranging illustrations or memory devises in sequence and carving them on cedar poles was the nearest approach the natives of the Northwest Coast had to writing.

In the chapters to follow, enough of the information required to enable one to identify many totem poles is given and a few of the better-known totem poles will be read.

Chapter Six

SOCIAL AND POLITICAL ORGANIZATION

In none of the tribes inhabiting the Northwest Coast of America was there any organization comparable to a nation. This was due in part to the character of the inhabitants who were intensely jealous of power, and partly due to their island and mountain terrain which made communications hazardous and therefore, infrequent. The word, *Tlingit*, like *Haida* and *Tsimshian* signified *the people* and was simply a linguistic grouping. Beyond language differences there was little to distinguish a Tlingit from a Haida or a Tsimshian. Physically they diverged so slightly that an outsider would be unable to discern any differences in these three northern tribes unless it was that on the average the Haidas are somewhat lighter complexioned and were when first discovered. Even this difference was heightened at an early date by intermingling with Europeans and Polynesians.

Those to the south, that is, the Kwakiutl, Bella Coola and Nootka also diverged but little from each other yet were darker and more squat than their northern brethren. Besides, some of these tribes practiced head-binding and flattening which produced an artificial distinction from their Alaskan cousins whose only mutilation was due to the use of huge lip ornaments or labrets by the women.

There were so many cultural exchanges between the three northern tribes that their literature, art, religion, architecture, clothing (including ceremonial garb), food, canoes, houses, weapons, and fishing gear were almost identical. Even language differences proved no great barrier to social life, and inter-marriage between members of different linguistic groups was frequent.

No leader ever rose up that was powerful enough to impose his will or leadership over an entire linguistic group. Hence, there was never such a thing as a war between all of the Haidas and all of the Tsimshians or Tlingits, and taxes or tribute was unknown. In fact, neither were the Russians ever able to collect tribute from them, and could pose as conquerors in the Totempolar Region only from safe positions behind their barricades at Sitka and Wrangell where they were virtual prisoners. For these were warlike people, well-equipped to fight terrestrial or marine battles on the home front with anyone. However, they had always confined their fighting to local feuds in which they required no allies. When the Russians came to stay in 1799, the Sitka Ravens sought to expel them single-handed and almost succeeded. But without the help of the local Wolf phratry, particularly the warlike Kag-wan-ton clan, they were doomed to failure and the invaders from Siberia took over.

AUKE CHIEF KOW-EE (Kow-wah-ee). Kow-ee, Chief of the Raven Phratry, Auke Tlingit Indians, was born about 1817 and died at Juneau on Feb. 27, 1892. Four days later he was cremated near the mouth of Gold Creek, at the approximate site of the monument commemorating the event. The woman at the left, wearing a silver labret in her lip, is Kow-ee's wife, *Ok-lak.* The other woman is Ok-lak's sister. Kow-ee wears epaulets which distinguish him as a Territorial Indian Policeman.

The strongest political group on the Northwest Coast was the village. This in turn had its strength and origin in a still more important basic group, the clan. An Indian clan may be defined as a group of people bound together by tradition of first ancestors and on this coast generally implies an early migration. The dominant clan in the village was headed by the leading house chief of that particular clan who, in times of war or when other important decisions were to be made, was accepted as leader, pro tem, by all the clans represented in the village. Thus, in Klukwan, the *Kagwanton* clan ruled, in Sitka it was the *Kiksadi,* and in Wrangell, the *Nanyaayi.*

The Tlingit and Haida were further divided into two matrilineal, exogamic phratries or totem groups. In plain language, this meant that descent was reckoned from the mother's side only, and one was obliged to marry outside of that line of ancestry. In fact, for a person to marry anyone bearing his totem was considered incestuous, even today. On the other hand, marriage to a first cousin on the father's side was considered ideal since no blood ties were recognized on that side.

In the Tlingit tribe, the phratry divisions are *Raven* and *Wolf* and in the Haida group they are *Raven* and *Eagle.* However, the Haida *Raven* equates with the Tlingit *Eagle,* while the Haida *Eagle* corresponds to the Tlingit *Raven.* There is considerable evidence known to physical anthropologists that these two phratries or brotherhoods were at one time distinct races or physical types and that the Tlingit *Ravens* were occupying the area alone when the people bearing the *Wolf* totem arrived. They apparently entered the region from the Interior by way of the larger river valleys like the Copper, Alsek, Taku, Stikine and Skeena and to have intermarried with the people found in residence there. In any event, their legends have it that upon arriving from the Interior, in some cases having to go under glaciers that bridged the rivers, they found the coastland already occupied by *Ancient Alaskans* (their term) and settled among them peaceably.

The Tsimshian had four phratry divisions whose totems were the *Grisly Bear, Raven, Wolf,* and *Eagle.* Since the Grisly Bears and Ravens were arranged for marriage purposes opposite the Wolves and Eagles, there were actually only two marriage groups as with the Tlingit and Haida. The Tsimshian Bear and Wolf agreed with the Haida Raven, while their Raven and Eagle corresponded with the Haida Eagle.

Under this phratry system, a child was born into the totem of his mother, that is, became upon birth a member of her division, and was required, when the time came, to contract marriage outside that group. In other words, a Tlingit boy whose mother was *Raven,* was a *Raven* and was required to marry an *Eagle.* His father, being an *Eagle* and therefore of the opposite totem did not raise his own son. So, at an early age the boy went to live in the household of his most promising maternal uncle, who, would also be a *Raven.* Upon the death of his uncle, the young man would inherit the estate that he had helped his uncle accumulate. He would also inherit his uncle's name and position and obligations, including wives. Where there was a great disparity in their ages, the nephew could choose a younger wife later on so that he could raise a family of his own but he would continue to provide

66

for his inherited wife until her death. The nephew was obliged to erect a memorial pole to the memory of his deceased uncle within the year and did not come into full possession of his uncle's rank and estate until this had been accomplished.

Membership in either the Raven or Wolf phratry did not imply that one was restricted to the phratry crest alone. Each clan, besides its phratry emblem had the use of several others, some of which they considered more important than the basic one. For example, the Tlingit Raven *Kiksadis* considered the Frog as their distinguishing crest because of an incident in the life of one of their clan progenitors. This made *Frog* their exclusive clan symbol and since it was not to be shared with other clans under *Raven* they made the most of it. The Wolf *Nanyaayi* clan considered the Grisly Bear and later, the Killerwhale to be more distinctive of their group than the phratry symbol, Wolf. On the other hand, the Wolf *Kagwanton* clan displayed the Wolf emblem more than any of the others that they had a right to, including the Shark, Grisly Bear, Killerwhale and Eagle.

The same applied even more so to the Haidas. Under both the Eagle and Raven totems were thirty-odd emblems, the same often being shared by both phratries. It was not uncommon to see an Eagle wearing a Raven design on his blanket or carving it on his totem pole. This was made possible in instances wherein fathers, although of the opposite phratry to their sons, would sometimes confer upon them, names and symbols that properly would have gone to a nephew. Crests sometimes got out of their original phratry and even tribe in instances wherein a Tsimshian chief might give or lose to a Haida chief one of his most valued crests. In this way one Haida clan achieved the *Mountain Goat* totem, although the mountain goat is nowhere to be found in Haida territory. The *Killerwhale* emblem of the Nanyaayi clan at Wrangell was won in battle from a *Niska* (Nass River Tsimshian) chief, *We-shakes*. One Tlingit-speaking clan, the *Nexadi*, was member of neither the Raven nor Eagle phratry and could therefore marry into either group, yet used the Eagle as its crest.

Besides being a member of a linguistic group, a phratry and a clan, Indians of these three northern tribes also belonged to a named community house group headed by a house chief. It is conceivable

THE ABRAHAM LINCOLN TOTEM POLE. The Lincoln totem pole was erected shortly after the purchase on Tongass Island near Alaska's southern border. Here a small garrison of soldiers manned Fort Tongass and the revenue cutter *Lincoln* was based to intercept smugglers and keep the peace. A small band of Tlingit seeking sanctuary from another band with whom they were feuding, learned about Lincoln and new white man's laws ending slavery. In gratitude they erected a memorial to the man responsible for their new security, Abraham Lincoln. Lincoln was carved with amazing realism by a professional Tsimshian carver named *Thle-da*, apparently from a Brady photograph, #48 in Meserve's Enumeration, showing Lincoln at Antietam.

The pole at the left is said to be the memorial to Chief Ebbets who was responsible for having the other poles carved. His pole is surmounted by his totem, the Raven, shown here with beak pointing upward. The small figure carved on Raven's breast appears to be Raven in human form. The lower figure is Black Bear, between whose ears a frog's head is seen.

The original Lincoln figure shown in this picture is preserved in the State Museum in Juneau.

built to accommodate them. These secondary houses built to house the overflow would have names, sometimes different from the original, and have separate house chiefs who would be considered sub-chiefs of the clan.

At the turn of the century at Wrangell, the Kiksadi clan had three houses, the Qatcadi had five and the Nanyaayi had six. Other clans represented there had from one to four houses each. At Sitka, the Kiksadi had seven houses and the Kagwanton at least sixteen. Among the Chilkats, the Ganaxadi clan had six houses and the Kagwanton eight.

Each house was named, the name being derived generally from one of the clan emblems. Thus, there was the Raven House, Grisly Bear House, Wolf House, Shark House, Big House, Bark House, Worm House and many others. Among the Tlingit, there were perhaps no more than fourteen original clans, the rest being affiliates or offshoots of the original fourteen.

Belonging to a clan or a house group did not necessarily imply that one was highborn for there were servant class clans and some entire groups were considered little more than slaves by the others.

All Indians of the Northwest Coast were graded socially into four classes, roughly comparable to royalty, nobility, commonalty and slaves. The highest order consisted of the chiefs and their first nephews who would succeed them. Next to them were the younger nephews and their families and people who had distinguished themselves in some way. Wealth and nobility were almost synonymous, and since a commoner, through the accumulation of wealth could rise to a higher social station, industry and planning were accelerated and rivalry was intense. The common people as ever made up the bulk of the population. These were free men related by blood to the nobility but unfortunately, poor and undistinguished. A third of the population consisted of slaves who had no status or rights and were regarded merely as chattels. This group consisted of men and women born in slavery, those acquired from neighboring tribes by purchase, and those captured in war or in slave raids generally conducted in the Puget Sound country. *Flathead* and *slave* were synonymous to these Northern tribes who did not practice headflattening themselves. The hair of slaves were kept short so that free men could recognize them and know how to address them.

In spite of these definite social distinctions, all classes lived under the same roof in the community house which could be compared to a roofed village with a communal fire. The chief's immediate family

THE OLD AND THE NEW. A Lighthouse Beacon or "Blinker" marks tortuous Sukkwan Narrows, where once tall totem poles stood guard. The hexagonal pole in the background is actually the "Fireweed Pole," symbolizing a Haida crest.
(Photo by the author).

that originally all members of a clan residing in a certain village occupied the same community house for these buildings were sometimes of huge dimensions. This household would be presided over by the head man or patriarch of that particular clan. But as the household expanded in the village or into other localities, additional houses had to be occupied a section at the rear of the house and enjoyed some privacy behind a painted heraldic screen or partition. Flanking the chief's apartment were those of the nobility, separated from each other by curtains of cedarbark matting. Less desirable quarters, on from two to three levels reached by ladders, went to commoners, while the slaves who did the drudgery of the household had no quarters but slept where they could in the drafts and damp at the entrance where they would be the first victims of a surprise attack on the house by enemies.

The Kwakiutls when first studied, were living under a social organization that agreed partly with that of the Haida and Tsimshian and partly with that of the Coast Salish and Nootka. Apparently the system was originally like that of their southern neighbors, but close association with the Tsimshian led the northern branch to embrace the matrilinear system whereas the southern branch remained patrilinear, that is, recognizing descent through the father only, or to recognize descent in both the male and female lines. In other words, a Kwakiutl child was not born into a clan but at a later date could be taken into the clan of either of its parents. Under this arrangement a Kwakiutl would try to marry well so that his offspring would thus become eligible to membership in an important clan. These clans attached great importance to their crests which they displayed either as paintings on their housefronts or as totem poles. The crest itself was supposed to represent a diety who, coming to earth and taking human form, had become the ancestor of the clan. Like their northern neighbors, marriage was prohibited between members of the same clan.

The Bella Coola, who were a branch of the Salish stock, yet hemmed in on all sides by the Kwakiutl, derived most of their customs from their near neighbors. They had no phratries but a number of clans claiming descent from mythological ancestors. Since membership carried with it property rights, historic names, rights to symbols, ceremonies and dances, there was a tendency to discourage marriage outside the clan for such action would eventually lessen and diffuse the accumulated wealth and privileges of the group. Hence descent through the male line was stressed rather than through the mother. Class lines were not tightly drawn and by achieving wealth any man not a slave could rise to become one of the society of chiefs who controlled the activities of the tribe.

The Nootka figured descent through either line although the eldest son took membership in his mother's clan if it happened to be more important or powerful than that of his father. The father was privileged to will certain rights or privileges either to his own children or to those of his sister.

The Nootka were considerably influenced by their neighbors, the Kwakiutl and the Bella Coola but little or no influence was exerted directly by the Tsimshian and Haida, their neighbors to the north. Like all other coastal tribes of this area they too, practiced slavery.

The Nootka tribe is the only one in the Northwest Coast culture area that hunted whales, but among them only the chiefs enjoyed the privilege of harpooning the whale. They did not carve tall totem poles like their northern neighbors but from the earliest times are known to have carved their tribal crests on the interior posts of their community houses. (See chart of the sub-divisions of the Tlingit attached)

THE CHILKAT BLANKET. Actually, a robe to be worn over the shoulders, this was a textile produced by a basket-weaving technique. The material was mountain goat wool and cedar bark on which the wool was wrapped to give it body. Original dyes were from a lichen (Evernia vulpina) for the yellow, equisetum root, and later hemlock bark boiled in an iron pot for the black. The green used in some blankets was derived from copper. Commercial dyes and even commercial wool cheapened many of the later blankets that were made for the tourist trade. A very few are still being made by Chilkat Tlingits at Klukwan and at no other place although they originated in prehistoric times with the Tsimshian.

This particular blanket, now in the State Museum at Juneau, depicts a diving whale in the center panel. Ravens face it from both side panels.

SUBDIVISIONS OF TLINGIT-SPEAKING PEOPLE
[ABBREVIATED]

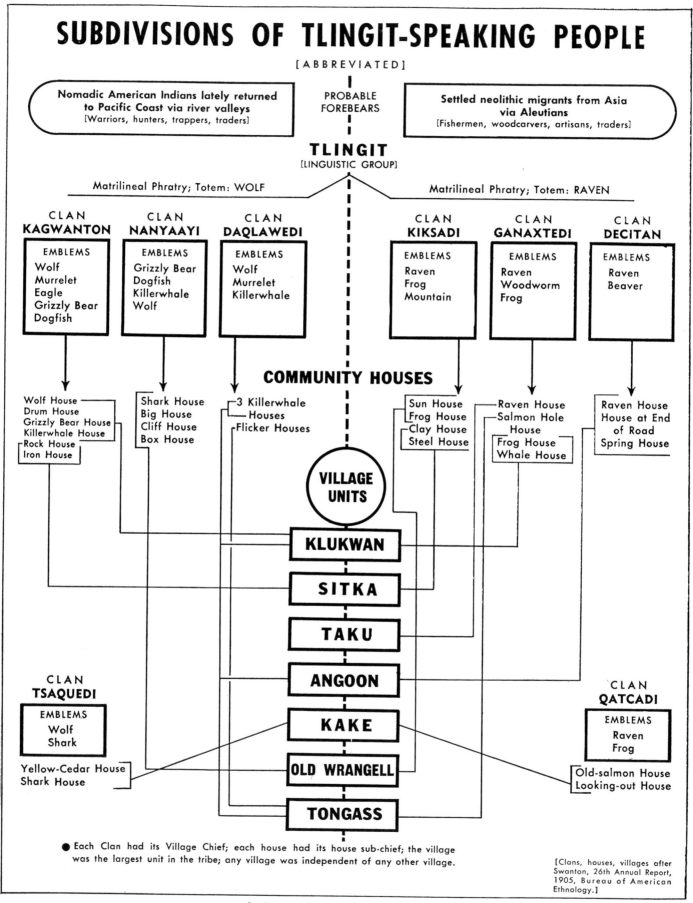

PROBABLE FOREBEARS

Nomadic American Indians lately returned to Pacific Coast via river valleys
[Warriors, hunters, trappers, traders]

Settled neolithic migrants from Asia via Aleutians
[Fishermen, woodcarvers, artisans, traders]

TLINGIT
[LINGUISTIC GROUP]

Matrilineal Phratry; Totem: WOLF

Matrilineal Phratry; Totem: RAVEN

CLAN KAGWANTON
EMBLEMS
Wolf
Murrelet
Eagle
Grizzly Bear
Dogfish

CLAN NANYAAYI
EMBLEMS
Grizzly Bear
Dogfish
Killerwhale
Wolf

CLAN DAQLAWEDI
EMBLEMS
Wolf
Murrelet
Killerwhale

CLAN KIKSADI
EMBLEMS
Raven
Frog
Mountain

CLAN GANAXTEDI
EMBLEMS
Raven
Woodworm
Frog

CLAN DECITAN
EMBLEMS
Raven
Beaver

COMMUNITY HOUSES

Wolf House
Drum House
Grizzly Bear House
Killerwhale House
Rock House
Iron House

Shark House
Big House
Cliff House
Box House

3 Killerwhale Houses
Flicker Houses

Sun House
Frog House
Clay House
Steel House

Raven House
Salmon Hole House
Frog House
Whale House

Raven House
House at End of Road
Spring House

VILLAGE UNITS

KLUKWAN

SITKA

TAKU

ANGOON

KAKE

OLD WRANGELL

TONGASS

CLAN TSAQUEDI
EMBLEMS
Wolf
Shark

Yellow-Cedar House
Shark House

CLAN QATCADI
EMBLEMS
Raven
Frog

Old-salmon House
Looking-out House

● Each Clan had its Village Chief; each house had its house sub-chief; the village was the largest unit in the tribe; any village was independent of any other village.

[Clans, houses, villages after Swanton, 26th Annual Report, 1905, Bureau of American Ethnology.]

Chapter Seven

NORTHWEST COAST ART

Since the Indians on the Northwest Coast were rain foresters as well as marine fishermen, the men's art was expressed primarily in wood sculpture and in the decoration of objects made of wood. They did, however, work in the medium of stone, bone, antler and horn, applying the wood carver's technique. Their art is symbolic, yet on occasion realism is employed, demonstrating that it is well within their capabilities.

The unusual characteristics of their art are what distinguished it from that of any other people in the world. One acquainted with this unique style can identify Northwest Coast art work instantly, wherever encountered and in whatever medium.

A prime prerequisite of all Northwest Coast art is that it serve a useful end. In other words, a useful object such as a spoon, dish, drum, box, paddle or weapon is made, then it is completely decorated. Hence, the artist is always restrained by the size and shape of the object to be decorated. This has led to an almost complete disregard for perspective and has introduced the qualities of dissection, rearrangement of parts, and distortion. In carving a totem pole, he is restricted by form of the log which is a gradually-tapering cylinder. If a frog is to appear below a bear it will bulk larger than the bear. If carved in proper perspective it might necessitate practically severing the pole at that place or leaving a large, undecorated area. But much worse, it would insult the frog since it is a symbol fully as important as the bear. Hence, on a totem pole, position of the figures displayed had considerable bearing on the size they would assume, as well as their importance in the narrative.

Since articles in daily use were often decorated in the totem or clan symbols of the owner, the artist was confronted with the problem of making a given symbol fit a space of any shape. Thus a raven had to be made circular to decorate a hat, drum, or a round dish, but rectangular to decorate a box or chest and lance-shaped to decorate a paddle. This was accomplished by distortion. Certain parts were greatly enlarged, others surpressed, bent or folded until the proper form was achieved. Balanced designs used on boxes, blankets, and heraldic screens were much in favor, and to achieve them the artist employed dissection. The so-called double-headed eagles and ravens were not actually double-headed at all since nothing of the kind appears in the native mythology or lore. These clan symbols had been simply split down the back and laid open to achieve a design which would be in perfect balance.

If the parts of the totemic symbol being employed in decoration failed to fit, they were

CHIEF SHAKES VII, WEARING CHILKAT BLANKET. He enters his restored Community House on Shakes Island, Wrangell Harbor, before erection of false front. The heavy cedar timbers and planks have been finished with the native adze which gives them a hammered-brass effect.

Photo by author.

removed, figuratively, and rearranged at the artist's pleasure. A common dogfish shark design employed on blankets reveals that the dogfish had first been decapitated, the body split along the spine, laid open, the head then being placed in the center. But that was not all. The eyes were next removed and placed above the mouth, for otherwise they could not be seen since a shark has its eyes on top, and mouth beneath, the head. Next, a nose was placed between the eyes and mouth while the snout became a high forehead above a somewhat human face. The true nostrils became mere decorations on the forehead, and were accompanied by a series of crescents which once were gillslits but degenerated to mere recognition features.

Since realism was seldom employed, a system of symbols was evolved by which the various figures could be recognized. This was achieved by taking some salient feature of the totem animal and stressing it. In the case of totem birds and clan symbols such as the eagle, raven, crane and hawk, beak differences were enough to make distinction easy, so the realistic bill became the recognition feature or *symbol* of the bird. The frog, actually a toad, is carved realistically but may be further identified by its toothless mouth, tailless body and three toes. The beaver is shown with two prominent incisors, a hachured tail, and often with a stick in its forepaws or mouth. The bear is generally quite realistic, but its large nostrils, paws, and fangs are the features. It is sometimes shown with a protruding tongue but so is the wolf. The wolf is shown in sculptures much like the bear but may be distinguished from the latter by its longer and sharper muzzle and elevated snout. Sometimes a long tail is carved running up the spine which helps to identify it since bear is characteristically carved, tailless. A pair of sharp horns serves to identify mountain goat whose cleft hoof is carved as a foot with two toes.

The killerwhale may be recognized from its prominent dorsal fin, the sculpin or bullhead by its large head, mouth turned up at the corners and the two spines above its eyes. The dogfish shark has gill slits shown as crescents, a crescent-shaped mouth depressed at the corners and filled with sawtooth-like teeth. Its unusual tail is generally realistic. The halibut differs from other fish in that it has a continuous fin and both eyes on one side. The octopus is shown with a bird-like head and

72

hooked bill (which it actually has) but the distinguishing features are the suction plates and tentacles.

Insects are sometimes hard to recognize since they are carved as conventionalized birds, the mosquito being sometimes mistaken for the crane. Close inspection will reveal that it has but one mandible. Unaccountably, the Haida artist depicts the mosquito with a coiled proboscis as if he intended a butterfly. The dragonfly is depicted with an abnormally large head, segmented body and paired wings. Except for the oversized head and noncompound eyes, it is quite realistic and would never be mistaken for anything else. The woodworm also has a segmented body but the absence of wings makes it readily distinguishable from the dragonfly.

Supernatural birds and animals generally are adaptations of known local species. Thus the Kwakiutl Thunderbird resembles the eagle while the Haida Thunderbird is more similar to the hawk although some of the carvers seemed to have had the albatross in mind. The Tlingit *Kadjuk*, a fabled bird of the mountains is definitely based on the golden eagle.

The Tlingit *Gonakadet* and its Haida equivalent, *Wasgo* has several forms but usually it is a combination of a wolf and a killerwhale. The sea grisly is carved like a bear with the addition of fins at the elbows and heels. In general, sea animals have round eyes, all others have eyes consisting of two outer curves, the upper one longer than the lower, inclosing a circle which represents the eyeball. Around this is carved a kidney-shaped area that is depressed and generally painted blue-green.

Women are distinguished from men by the pres-

KAKE TOTEM POLES. The men in the foreground dressed as Indian chiefs are not Indians. The one in the Chilkat blanket is Fred Sepp, early Kake trader and beside him is Ernest Kirberger, his partner. The totem poles were presumably destroyed in 1912 and Kirberger's Tlingit collection burned with his store in 1926.

The alligator-like animal on the pole to the right is the Land Otter and the one in the middle with a goat-like head is *Bullhead* or *Sculpin*, the horn-like protuberances being spines. Above it, looking like a unicorn is Eagle. The small shaft above its head may once have supported a small flag. The bottom figure on the pole to the left is probably *Octopus*.

Case & Draper.

PICTOGRAPHS IN RED OCHRE (Hetta Inlet). Records of a mysterious band, these cliff paintings have nothing in common with the art style of the Northwest Coast, yet are not as old as the "battered" petroglyphs which have an unmistakeable affinity with it.

(Photo by the author).

Note: Outlines were traced with clamshell since paintings were too faint to photograph otherwise. (ELK)

PETROGLYPHIC GONAKADET CARRYING WHALE (Hetta Inlet). Probably the earliest representation of the monster known to the Tlingit as "Gonakadet" and to the Haida as "Wasgo," this is the same supernatural being that appears on the "Old Witch" totem and on the smaller of the Kadashan totems as well as the mortuary to the left of Shakes' door.

(Photo by author).

ence of a labret in the lower lip of the women, otherwise they are similar. Sex parts are seldom, if ever, encountered in totem poles or any other art work of the Northwest Coast Indians although some phallic stone implements are found in the area now occupied by them that no doubt were made by their ancestors.

The native artist seemed at all times to have been conscious of the skeletal form of his subject. Thus, he symbolized each joint with an *eye* form that may have been derived from a ball and socket joint. But if the joint to be depicted is large, the eye became a face. He abhorred vacant spaces as well as straight lines and sharp angles so in drawing a whale he would indicate the backbone as well as the ribs with symbols. Vertebra were fairly realistic but intersperced with the eye symbol representing joints, the ribs themselves appearing as reverse curves, in a quasi-xray composition. The otherwise bare abdomen of the beaver is often filled by its cross-hatched tail and the tail of a whale is also drawn up on its belly occasionally just to fill the space. In most cases, however, vacant spaces are filled with eyes or the conventional *flicker-feather* design in one or more of its many forms.

One of the most mysterious practices of the Northwest Coast artist was his use of ears, placed prominently on the heads of both animals and birds, alike. Human beings are depicted with realistic ears at the sides of the head, yet supernatural people are shown with the conventional ear at the top of the head as in animals. This *ear*, if it is an ear, is in the form of the *flicker-feather*, the most

prominent feature in all Northwest Coastal art. It is used as a feather or scale design; as an ear or a fin or simply as a space filler. It is most versatile for it may be short and thick, long and slender, curled, distorted, embellished in a hundred different ways. It is possible that originally the *ear* was simply a *plume*, doubled for balance, the plume being the black-edged tail feather of the red-shafted flicker, common throughout the area.

In at least one old myth, a salmon was identified as being supernatural because it had a red feather in its head. It may have been the practice of early carvers to place the *plume* on the head to distinguish supernatural animals from the common variety as high caste people may have worn a feather to distinguish them from the commoners. In any event, ordinary people are depicted with realistic ears while supernatural people often are shown with the flicker feather ear while others have both. Whales are not shown with ears but in their case the pectoral fins occupy the position of ears in the carvings and double for them since they, too, carry the flicker feather design.

Since birds, insects, fish and animals are regarded as people, capable of taking human form at will, they are often depicted as human beings. However, there will always be something to designate what was intended. Raven may be shown in human form but with a raven's wings worn like an overcoat or with a human body and a raven's head. A whale might have a human face but will have in addition, a blow-hole in the forehead. Dogfish sharks sometimes are shown with human faces but with gillslit symbols in the cheeks. A squid or devil-fish might appear as a human being but with tentacle suckers in the position of eyebrows.

With the advent of white men on the Northwest Coast, things began to appear on totem poles for which there were no symbols or conventionalized forms, hence realism was employed. Russians were generally shown with full black beards and European dress; Lincoln was undoubtedly copied from a Brady photograph; steamboats appear with funnel and sidewheels. This was no tax on the abilities of the artist, however, since portraiture had long been practiced in the making of realistic masks, headdresses, and heads used in ceremonies wherein decapitation was feigned.

Like the totem pole sculpture, the decorative art of the Northwest Coast as we know it is recent. Many museum pieces in stone and wood reveal that the artist of this region had not always favored the curvilinear figures he executed to the exclusion of all others. Food and storage boxes in particular were formerly decorated with plain geometric figures, and red was the only color employed on them. The women's art as seen in mats and baskets was also formal and meaningless, except that the various designs employed had names. In fairly recent times, however, the native women have been prevailed upon by whites to imitate the men's totemic figures on their baskets.

The Chilkat goat-wool blanket or robe was, of course, symbolic and according to the Northwest Coast decorative art style. But this was not an example of the women's art even though women made the blankets. They were merely copying designs painted on the pattern boards by male designers who, naturally, followed their style rather than that of the women.

Totem poles were painted with a type of fish-egg tempera, consisting of a pulverized mineral pigment mixed with a vehicle of masticated fresh salmon eggs and saliva. The colors that endured were originally red, black and apple green, according to several early informants and objects collected at a very early date. The red was obtained from hematite, rarely cinnabar, the black from local graphite deposits and soot. Various shades of blue and green or blends described as apple green came from copper earths common throughout the region. For many years commercial paints have been used but none have achieved the soft, flat tones of the native paints seen today only in a few well-preserved interior house pillars. As early as the 18th century, dry pigments were traded to the totem carvers and the *lively red* seen by Meares and others was probably British vermilion mixed with local hematite to produce a brighter red and at the same time eke out the expensive imported pigment.

One of the most interesting features of the decorative art of the Tlingit, and to some extent their neighbors, was the use of human hair in their ceremonial objects. Human hair was used not only in masks but to provide fringes for their chief's staffs and song leader's batons. Certain figures on house pillars and heraldic screens were given real hair and it was also used to ornament small objects such as rattles and figurines.

Although in most instances the hair actually enhanced the object in which it was set, that was not the primary reason for putting it there. Actually, the hair was that of their own beloved dead. By using it to ornament ceremonial objects it was their belief that the dead were thereby enabled to share in the happiness of the occasions when these objects were used or displayed.

GONAKADATE PILLAR AND DUK-TOOLH PILLAR. Two of the four interior house pillars of the Whale House at Klukwan, Alaska where they may still be seen in their original Indian paint.
(Photo from Emmons' The Whale House of the Chilkat.)

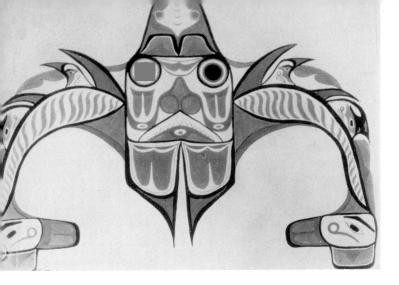

DISSECTED SHARK DESIGN. To make a balanced design, the fish has been decapitated, split asunder, the head replaced at the center. Eyes have been moved to underside, new nostrils added. Snout has now become a vaulted forehead with original nostrils merely a decorative feature. The gill-slits, which are a recognition feature, have been moved to the forehead where they appear as a row of crescents.

(Photo by author).

A CLOSE-UP OF A BEAVER'S TAIL. Revealing methods of carving and repair. Here the hachured tail is drawn up against the belly; the face represents the joint.

The belief in the magical power of human hair is demonstrated in two canoe figures on display in the State Museum at Juneau. In this case, the hair of two slain chiefs was inserted in the heads of the canoe figures to give the canoe *spirit*. The shaman rode in this canoe which headed an expedition undertaken to avenge the killing of the above chiefs several years earlier.

Proof that the hair used in ceremonial objects came from relatives and not from slaves or enemies is demonstrated in a baton kept by a Tlingit family of Kake. In this instance the hair was red and is displayed on auspicious occasions as proof of a distinguished lineage.

In decorating wooden objects with hair, the usual procedure followed by Tlingit artisans was to drill a series of small holes at uniform distances apart, varying from a quarter inch to two inches or so, depending on the object. The tuft of hair to be inserted in the hole was first bent in the middle across the blunt end of a short wooden peg which, when driven in flush, held the tuft upright securely. When properly set, all were clipped to a uniform length. These clipped tufts appear so coarse and

A TWO-HEADED BOY. One wonders if such a boy actually lived since no legend that has survived in the native oral literature mentions such a being, supernatural or otherwise. The carving was given to Barrett Willoughby, famous Alaskan novelist, by a sea captain when she was a small girl. Made of alder in Haida style, it could have been carved by a Tlingit some place where yellow cedar didn't grow and alder was substituted.

HAIDA CIRCULAR DESIGN. Depicting sculpin (bullhead) suitable for hat or bowl. Spines above nostrils are the recognition features.

(Photo by author).

bristly that they have sometimes been described as *horse tail* which they resemble very closely but laboratory tests revealed their true nature.

In decorating ceremonial batons in the typical killerwhale-fin and canoe paddle designs, the hair fringe appears along the back edge only. In this instance, the hair is not clipped but drapes gracefully, the locks being six or more inches in length.

HAIDA PAINTINGS. Of "Was-go" or the "Gonakadet" referring to the same myth as that of the Hetta Inlet petroglyph. The young man who dressed in the gonakadet's hide is here shown crouching in its mouth and is in the act of bringing in the two whales that caused his death. (See Gonakadet Story)

(Photo by author).

CHIEF SHAKES VII. Last of a long line of Nanyaayi Chiefs of the Wrangell and Stikine Tlingits, Chief Shakes VII (Kudanake) died Jan. 16, 1944.

Photo by author (1940).

KWAKIUTL HOUSE IN THUNDERBIRD PARK, VICTORIA, B.C. This is an authentic replica of a Kwakiutl Indian community house that was built at Fort Rupert about one hundred years ago. The only difference is that the original was twice as big as this replica. Built by Chief *Naka'penkin,* the ancestor of Carver Mungo Martin, its name was *Wa'waditla.* The design on the front of the house is *Tsee'akis,* a supernatural bullhead or sculpin. This replica was designed by Mungo Martin, famous Kwakiutl carver.

British Columbia Government Photo.

Chapter Eight

NORTHWEST COAST RELIGION

As the Northwest Coast emerged from the Glacial Age, nature in all its moods conspired to impress the earliest inhabitants with their utter helplessness in the hands of their Creator. Wild and stormy seas threatened them on the one hand, dark, impenetrable forests, lofty, forbidding mountains and chill, impassable glaciers and rivers on the other. Ferocious wolves and man-killing bears shared the forest with a host of still more dreaded demons of their imagination. Weird, croaking ravens and sinister owls staring at them from dripping trees contributed to the awfulness of the land.

Lacking even an elementary knowledge of science, these isolated men sought to explain things that they did not understand, as man has the world over, by accounting for them as *supernatural*. They brought themselves to believe that all things about them were possessed of spirits having the power to help or harm them either here or in the *hereafter*. To propitiate these powerful unseen beings and otherwise secure their goodwill was the basis of their religion, and the acts of propitiation were directed toward the spirit believed capable of doing the most evil. This has led some early writers to classify the natives of the Totempolar region as devil-worshippers. This, obviously, was untrue for these simple folk did not worship evil beings—they simply attempted to safeguard their families from occult forces by a policy of appeasement.

As a matter of fact, none of these tribes worshipped anything, nor did they offer any sacrifices. They lacked an organized priesthood, had no houses of worship, no idols, and no congregational worship. Yet, in spite of the lack of all these embellishments of simple faith, they were intensely religious.

Religious acts consisted largely of the observance of numerous taboos. Origin of the several *thou shalt nots* can be traced to myths that have been handed down by word of mouth from time immemorable. Since these myths will be treated in another chapter they will not be discussed here. Suffice that it was through the myths that they learned that animals were really people in disguise, some purposely taking the form of food animals so that man might be fed. Taboos relating to these beings were directed against improper handling, waste and hoarding. Salmon, for instance, were not allowed to be kept more than one year, not because it might spoil, but because the salmon was being deprived of its natural life. Its spirit could not be released to come to life in its own *country* until it had been eaten and the remains burned or thrown into the sea. Disregard of this taboo meant eventual starvation, for the salmon chief was sure to punish

79

KWAKIUTL GRAVE TOTEM AT ALERT BAY, B.C. (No longer standing).

(Photo by author).

the tribe by refusing to send them salmon the following season.

Since salmon was the staple food throughout the entire region, considerable effort was made to insure its continued supply. Supplications were addressed to the salmon chief in the form of petroglyphs or symbols graven on the rocks at the mouths of the sockeye salmon streams. These glyphs were pecked and battered in by slaves, and consisted of various symbols and figures representing first the group in possession of the stream, and second, beings known or believed to be in special favor with the salmon people. Myths, that later were used to embellish totem poles, were graven much earlier on the beach boulders, and hundreds of them may still be found in place, throughout the entire region.

Other myths continually reminded the people of the dire consequences of disrespectful acts, words or even thoughts directed against living beings or the dead. A woman who made a remark insulting to the bears in general was courted and married by a bear that had taken human form in order to deceive and punish her for her insults. Others had been punished similarly by the snails, devilfish and frogs. On the other hand the Indians were aided and rewarded by certain spirits, and ambitious men observed elaborate rites in order to secure these favors. Bathing, fasting, purging, and continence were the means of achieving spiritual favor for the spirits were believed to have an exceptionally keen sense of smell. A boy who had fasted until he was transparent was especially rewarded.

Ancestors were not worshipped but the dead were highly respected. This was because they believed that in the life which followed death their relatives were largely dependent on the acts of the living for their comfort and well-being. Hence, the Tlingit burned the dead so that they would be warm in the next world. They sang songs so that their way would be lighted, and they put food into the fire at periodic *feasts of the dead* in the belief that a little food offered thus would provide a great deal for the deceased relative to whom it was directed. In some instances slaves were killed, not as sacrifices, but to accompany their masters to the next world where they would continue to serve them as they had on earth. Grave houses are still to be seen furnished with *killed property* for the use of the dead in the spirit world.

The Tlingit's idea about the next world was reputedly derived from people who had returned from the dead. All people did not go to the same place as there seems to have been unseen worlds, none of them comparable to Heaven, on three different planes. One was similar to and on a level with this world; another was above and a third below. Those who died natural deaths went to a land similar to the one from which they had departed and there followed cheerless, uneventful lives. They plied their old tasks and those who in life had been rich on earth were still the ruling class. They were dependent as stated above, on the acts of their relatives and suffered greatly if forgotten or otherwise neglected. Warriors and people meeting violent death went to a special place in the sky where they were received with much rejoicing, but life there was much the same as it was on earth. Thieves and witches were sent below to a place resembling Hades. They believed in transmigration of souls for in some cases spirits, weary of life in spirit-land, returned to earth as newborn babes. Birthmarks and other signs were taken as indication of such occupancy and the child thus marked was named for the one whose spirit it was believed to possess.

The Haida believed that in death the *soul flies away* whereupon the dead man finds himself on a trail which he follows to the shore of a bay, across which lies the *Land of Souls*. A person carrying a red walking stick crosses the bay on a self-propelled raft and ferries the man across. Once in the Land of Souls the man starts a search for his wife but he has a hard time finding her since there are many villages. There is only one wife there, she being the first, in the event that he has had several. After a time he *dies again* or goes by canoe to another land called *Xada*. Three more lives and deaths follow in time, and eventually he returns to earth in the form of a blue fly.

Not all who die go to the Land of Souls. Those who have drowned go to the Killer Whale People under the sea. Those dying a violent death go to *Taxet's House* in the sky. Those who starve go to Greatest-Stingy-One's House. Those who fall to their deaths go to the House-Hanging-from-the-Shining-Heavens.

If the mother of the dead put a little food in the fire and pour a little water in a hole near the fire, a great quantity of each will go to her child in the Land of Souls. If she fails to do this the child

THE GRAVE OF KOW-ISH-TE (SHAKES V). During Kow-ish-te's Chieftainship, coastal Southeastern Alaska was leased by the Russians to the British, Redoubt St. Dionysius became Fort Stikine, and finally, Alaska having been purchased by the United States, the Stikine port became Fort Wrangell. His grave displays the Killer-Whale symbol won in battle by his ancestor, Gush-klin, from the Niska chief, We-Shakes. The name "Shakes," a corruption of "We-Shakes" was won in the same battle.

(Photo by the author).

SHAMAN TORTURING A SUS-PECTED WITCH. This Haida carving in alder depicts the first degree of torture exacted by the shaman to obtain a confession. Here the hands are seen bound and the neck is being twisted by a devil's club stick, thrust through a loop in the hair. If this fails, the head is drawn back and lashed to the wrists. No confession forthcoming, the head, hands, and feet are then bound together and in this position the suspected culprit is dropped into a pit under the floor. Salt water answers his pleas for a drink, and here he will remain until death or confession releases him. It is no wonder that suspected witches often confessed a guilt they didn't have.

will suffer from hunger and thirst.

The Haida conceived the earth to be flat, with rounded contour, over which hung a solid firmament like an inverted bowl. From this firmament were suspended the sun, moon, and stars, free to move about. These were inanimate although the sun and moon were inhabited by supernatural beings. The sun bulks far less in importance in the native mythology than the moon. Above the firmament was the abode of some of the supernatural beings.

Beneath the heavens were two islands: Haida-land and the mainland. The latter is known to be the larger although the sea was believed to slope away from Haida-land. This island rests on a great supernatural being called *Sacred-one-Standing-and-Moving.* He, in turn, rests upon his back on a copper box. It is his movements that cause earthquakes.

Supernatural beings were grouped in three general categories: Beings of the Upper World, Beings of the Sea, and Beings of the Land. Of the first group, somewhat apart from the rest, is *Sins-aga-nag-wai* who is the Haida equivalent of a *Supreme Diety.* According to some informants all spiritual beings receive their power from him. Man feels too humble to deal directly with this *God* but appeals to him indirectly through secondary dieties.

The Thunderbird, a mythical creature, was believed to produce thunder by rustling its feathers and lightning by blinking its eyes. It is not so important as a diety with the Haidas since in their country it seldom thunders. However, it enjoys a prominent place among the clan symbols, being depicted generally in the form of a hawk.

Also in the heavens are the abodes of several other supernatural beings whither go certain of the dead. The winds, particularly the prevailing South-eastern and the Northwest winds, were personified.

Since the Haida are primarily a maritime people, the Beings of the Sea were of great importance to them. Besides the ordinary creatures such as the killerwhales, salmon, herring, seals etc. there were many mythical beings, as well. The greatest of all the *Ocean People* are the *Killerwhale People.* Like their neighbors, the Tlingit, the Haida believed every animal was or might be the embodiment of a being who, at his own pleasure, could appear in human form. They were looked at from two distinct points of view: first, as animals that could be killed and eaten; second, as supernatural beings in disguise, when they would be spoken of as the *Salmon People, Herring People, Forest People* etc. As such they might entertain men in their towns, inter-marry with them, help or harm or punish them.

The *Ocean People* were believed to be divided into phratries and clans and to live like people in community houses and villages under the sea.

Of the *Land Beings,* there were those who dwelt in the earth, others in swamps, forests and lakes. But the most important were the *Creek Women* who live at the head of each stream. They own the fish and it is in the hopes of seeing her that the salmon periodically run up the streams. All die in the attempt save the steelheads and the trout who try again and again.

Other land beings are the Wood Creatures or *Forest People.* Every quadruped, bird or insect seems to have had a human form and the power to help or harm people. The taboo system was arranged by the Haida to promote social harmony between men and the *other people* used for food.

Besides these three main categories of supernatural beings there is a host of Patron Dieties such as a mythical bird called *Skil*, by hearing the call of which one would become wealthy. Another was *Property Woman* who, if seen would bestow wealth to the one seeing her or who heard her child cry. Some were good, other portend disaster or pestilence. Most of the supernatural beings are the property of the Raven phratry.

As in the case of the Tlingit, there is no priesthood among the Haida distinct from the Shamans or *Medicine Men*. Shamans got their power from supernatural beings who *possessed* them. In other words, it was believed that the *being* uses the shaman as a medium through which it communicates with the world of men. This calling was hereditary from maternal uncle to nephew. The nephew frequently acted as understudy and assistant to the Shaman who passed his *Spirits* and outfit on to his nephew when he felt death approaching. The young Shaman later acquires other spirits on his own, thereby gaining in power. The Haida Shaman dressed and wore a mask to correspond to the spirit he believed to be possessing him. If it happened to be a Tlingit spirit, he spoke in that tongue although he may have had no previous knowledge of that language. The principal supernatural beings who spoke through Shamans were the *Canoe People, Ocean People, Forest People* and the *Above People*. Either men or women served as Shamans.

Shamanism came to the Alaskan Indians as well as Eskimos from Asia where it had its origin among the Ural-Altaic peoples of Europe and Northern Siberia. In this faith an unseen world is conceived, in which there are gods, demons and ancestral spirits responsive mainly to Shamans, the priests or conjurers of Shamanism. The word *shaman* comes to us from the Tungusic *saman* which itself is derived from the Sanskrit.

Shaman is probably the first logical step towards an organized religion from the earlier form of worship practiced on the Northwest Coast known as *animism*. An *animist* believes all things to possess a soul or spirit which may help or aid one, on this earth or in the land of souls. The Indians of Southeastern Alaska and Coastal British Columbia were true animists in this respect, Shamanism differing only in that it went further, in providing the beginnings of a priesthood.

As stated earlier the profession passed from maternal uncle to nephew but this was not always the case. Anyone, including women, having an unusual experience with supernatural forces might take up the profession with common consent. Or persons afflicted with epilepsy, crossed eyes, red hair, double crown, or born with any other physical or mental divergence from the normal might be selected and trained from infancy for the profession. This training included long periods of self-denial, torture, bathing, fasting, retching and purging with native drugs, and nights spent in burial places. For the philosophy of Shamanism held that the Shaman was merely a mouthpiece through which the spirit voices spoke. In order to become acceptable as this mouthpiece, the potential Shaman must first attain purity and cleanliness, physical and spiritual, internal and external.

The work of a Shaman was varied and important to the tribe, and he was well paid and respected, often ranking next to the ruling chief in importance. In those days of the not too distant past, sickness was believed to be caused either by witchcraft or by losing the soul. In the first instance the Shaman was called upon to remove the offending object which had been placed in the victim by witchcraft, causing the malady, and then to ascertain and

THE KOOSHTA-KAH OR LAND OTTER MAN. This is still the bogey man of the Northwest Coast, and little children still see him on occasion, under canneries and other spooky places. But once he was the serious concern of everybody. People believed that lost men were converted into beings like this by land otters but by elaborate ritual could be redeemed to human status.

The Haidas tell the story of a slave who fled to an uninhabited islet from which he was unable to escape. Years later a party of marine hunters cruising by this islet saw a strange creature crawl out of the forest on hands and knees and down to the rocky beach. The tide being out, it proceeded to gnaw off mussels from the rocks with its teeth. When captured, the hunters recognized the escaped slave, now without clothing, scarred with devilclub thorns, emaciated and obviously insane. He was brought into the village and staked out as a reminder to the other slaves not to try to get away. When he died, a carving similar to this was made to serve the same purpose. This may have been the origin of the concept of the land otter men which are always shown on all fours, with lips curled back and teeth exposed.

KLINKWAN VILLAGE. The snow white Presbyterian Church in the background contrasts strangely with the decaying monuments in the fore. This view was taken in 1910 and an exodus to the new town of Hydaburg began shortly thereafter.

punish the witch. In the second case, his mission was to find the lost soul and restore it to its owner, whereupon the patient would immediately rise up, well and whole. He had also to accompany all war parties for although the warriors could kill the bodies of their enemies, the success of the venture was doubly assured if the Shaman first killed their souls, for the latter were believed to be of greater potential danger than the physical bodies.

The Haida believed that witches and wizards became such by being inhabited by mice, sometimes as many as ten. Friends of the accused helped them expel the mice, thus effecting a cure. Invariably the last mouse to be expelled was a white one. The Tlingit apparently never attempted to cure a witch but cruelly tortured them in order to exact a confession and to regain the charms by which the victim had been *witched*. The torture generally resulted in death for the alleged witch.

Raven or *Yethl* is the most important figure in the mythology of the three northern tribes and carries the role of *trickster diety*. While he is credited with having been the creator of the physical world, the Haidas believed *Sins-aga-nag-wai* had created life itself. Raven was a combination of good and bad traits: gluttonous, thieving, immoral and unfaithful in his dealings with his bird and animal associates, yet a great benefactor to the human race.

As can be inferred from the above, totem poles had less of a religious significance than social. They at no time had anything in common with idols and never were they worshipped nor did they figure in religious ceremonials. Mortuary poles were associated with religious concepts of death and life after death and many of the stories carved on totem poles figured in the religion of the country. But except for these two relatively unimportant rela-

tions they have no religious significance.

However, shortly after the purchase of Alaska, over-zealous and under-informed missionaries flocking into Alaska initiated a campaign to abolish totem poles and totem pole carving believing that they were pagan idols. Not content to allow the custom to die a natural death with the introduction of a superior religious philosophy they set about to destroy the totem poles already standing and were eminently successful in most instances. In Kake village, for an instance, virtually all of the totem poles were destroyed, apparently on the pretense that they were a menace to health. Many of them did contain charred bones of the dead but the real motive behind their destruction was to remove an important symbol of an allegedly unholy past.

The Reverend William Duncan, founder of Metlakatla, was just as successful in destroying this art and custom but more subtle in his methods. Among the fifteen pledges the members of his colony were required to observe were: to give up their Indian deviltry; to cease calling in conjurers (shamans) when sick; to cease giving away their property for display (potlatching); to attend religious instruction; to build neat homes.

These pledges spelled doom for the totem pole in general for Christian burial ended the need for the mortuary column; modern houses required no carved house posts nor pillars, and the ban on potlatching meant that none of those imposing monuments would ever again be erected by the Tsimshian of Metlakatla. New occupations introduced by Duncan such as lumbering, salmon canning, carpentry and boatbuilding replaced native crafts completely. It was not long before all other native communities in the region abandoned the old religious order as well as social customs almost entirely. Duncan's colony got away from the old influences by moving to an entirely new environment and the same effect was obtained in the various other villages when the inhabitants left them to live in the vicinity of canneries and in white men's towns where employment could be obtained.

All Indians in the Totempolar region now profess the Christian faith, and many have become successful and outstanding ministers of the Gospel to their own people. Yet a few Shamans still practice their occult art and a belief in witchcraft is still latent in most of the native villages.

Shortly after publication of the first edition of this book, the following letter was received from the Reverend George E. Beck, dean of Alaskan missionaries who recently departed this life at the age of 92. I am sure he would approve my publishing his letter which clarifies the matter of the destruction of the totem poles at Kake and throws much light on the position, the difficulties, and the problems of the pioneer missionaries on the Northwest Coast:

Ketchikan, Alaska
Jan. 22nd, 1946

Dear Mr. Keithahn:

Your letter of January 18th just received. Your book "Monuments in Cedar" was presented to me as a Christmas gift. As a book so well written, bound and printed I have enjoyed it very much. I shall not attempt to review or criticize it but shall endeavor to answer the questions asked. However, I must admit I am almost bitter on the subject of Indian Arts and Crafts as they are being forced back upon a worthy people who have outgrown them and are reaching out for better things.

The people of Alaska had reached a point where they realized their system of Government was not good. They were a clever people, able to maintain themselves under all conditions (if left alone). It came to them their whole system of Government was built on selfishness, supported on blackmail and founded on superstition and for this reason as the people progressed in the natural course of evolution, the age of the totem pole ended, they were either discarded or as at Kake destroyed. The people tried to forget and that is the main reason why it is hard to write an "Authentic Story of the Totem Pole": you cannot find two old men who will tell you the same story about any one pole.

After eighteen years on the faculty of the Sitka Training school, afterwards the Sheldon Jackson school, I was ordained by the Presbytery of Alaska and sent to Kake in the summer of 1912. Kake was about sixty-five miles by sea from the nearest peace officer or doctor. Mrs. Beck and I were met with black looks and all anyone would say was, "We don't know you; we will wait and see what you are going to do." All the people seemed greatly discouraged; their sidewalks and large tribal houses were falling to pieces; fighting and heavy drinking was the order of the day. The whites of the whole country round about were afraid of them. The Kake natives were unjustly blamed for the disappearance of any white man who happened to be shipwrecked or lost in that part of the country. The people were tired of their way of life and wanted to change.

There were many totem poles in Kake then; large crude affairs, and a number of so-called mortuary poles but as far as I could see there was nothing in them but just a handful of well-burnt ashes so there could be no question of burning them for sanitary reasons. The custom of cremation had been given up many years before I landed as can be proved by the great number of graves on the two islands just in front of the village when we arrived there in 1912.

Kake was about equally divided between the Salvation Army under the leadership of Charles Newton and his wife (as fine a young native couple as I ever met) and the Friends mission. The

THE TLINGIT CREMATED THEIR DEAD: with the exception of shamans. Since it was believed their bodies would not burn, they were embalmed by primitive means, wrapped in cedar bark shrouds, and placed on promontories under natural or contrived shelters.

CHIEF JOHNSON'S POLE. Probably the most photographed totem pole in Alaska, this is the first Alaska pole seen *in situ* by the author 40 years ago. This early view shows also a fine house painting of a stylized killer whale. The chief's new house in the background was no doubt influenced by that of Chief Kadashan who in 1887 put up a two-storey residence with four bay windows in Wrangell. (See story)

Case & Draper.

Friends church and mission buildings had just been sold to the Board of Home Missions of the Presbyterian Church without consulting the members of the church and they felt they had been sold out so my position in the village was anything but secure.

Charlie Gunnuk was the main leader of the Friends church and he was a very fine old gentleman. I am sure that neither he or the Friends church were the leaders in the burning of the poles. After a few months of hard work the leaders of both organizations came to me with this story and request. They said both the Salvation Army and the church have broken down, our people have become "backsliders." We are afraid, something must be done, we cannot do it alone. Will you help us and tell us what to do? Nothing was said about totem poles; they were a thing of the past; they did not enter into the picture either in the minds of Charles Newton, Charlie Gunnuk or my own. Many of the

poles were out of sight anyway, covered with brush and trees. We went to work. The people had a very able brass band but like everything else they had given up practice, and feasts for the dead and drunken dances had taken over everything.

I called a meeting of the whole town, told them the only practical way out was the spiritual life through Christ Jesus and then put on a regular political campaign. We turned out the band, nominated a large number of candidates and elected twelve men for a council and then the twelve men appointed a town marshal and city magistrate, built a jail and set the town on its feet. We asked the Governor of Alaska if we could be given any legal standing and he said, "you have no legal standing and can't be given any but there is such a thing as government with the consent of the governed and if the people want it that way, KEEP UP THE GOOD WORK and I will back you up if things

MODERN KWAKIUTL MEMORIAL POLES. In Alert Bay, B.C. Cemetery.

(Photo by author).

get out of hand."

All this time the poles were sleeping quietly in the brush. One morning I was awakened with the feeling that something unusual was taking place; rushing out I found the place covered with smoke and nearly all the poles blown up and burned. One pole was still standing in the churchyard. I asked what they were going to do with it. They said it is yours; do what you like with it; when I refused to touch it, they burned it with the rest. The whole village took part in the work but no one would admit giving the orders. They said they wanted to clean up and get rid of the old life that was not good. I have not kept a record of these doings but as the poles were all there in 1912 and gone in 1914 they must of burned in 1913.

And now comes the strange part of the story, but like everything else connected with the totem pole, I have nothing to prove it but I believe it to be true. There was living in Kake at that time an old Indian Doctor. The people had lost faith in him but he still held some power over them and sometime after the

burning of the poles I was told he could see the old life was changing; one after another the old customs were going out and unless he did something drastic he would go out with the rest of the old ways. So he told the people that his spirit had discovered an evil spirit lurking in the ashes of the departed in the old poles and unless they destroyed all of the totems the whole village would be wiped out. The people, having lost interest in the poles and wanting to get rid of them anyway, obeyed the doctor.

I have been so busy trying to lead this fine people out of the darkness they were in that I have spent very little time taking pictures. I have nothing on the Kake poles or any others; in fact, a missionary in those days was not supposed to have money enough to buy equipment and the powers that be saw to it that he did not have salary enough to lead him into temptation.

Very sincerely yours,
(signed) George E. Beck

87

TOTEMS OF OLD SUKKWAN. Marking site of deserted Haida Village soon to be reclaimed by the advancing spruce forest. Dozens of these poles are still to be seen in remote former village sites, too rotted to move.

(Photo by the author).

PETROGLYPHS ON BEACH AT WRANGELL. Hundreds of these battered and pecked rock pictures constitute the earliest form of art in the Totempolar Regions.

(Photo by the author).

Chapter Nine

NORTHWEST COAST ORAL LITERATURE

The unwritten literature of the Indians of the Northwest Coast consists of innumerable myths, legends, and tales handed down by word of mouth from generation to generation and from tribe to tribe for centuries, no doubt. Through the passage of time and from translation from language to language, original accounts have been altered in many ways. Some have become hopelessly involved, others garbled, some even embellished. Not a few have been expurgated since the arrival of missionaries and schoolteachers as some of the native tales would be obscene by our standards.

While all myths, since they deal with the action and activity of gods, supernatural beings and culture heroes, may be considered religious in character, they must also be viewed as literature since they were recited primarily to furnish amusement and entertainment. Raven's role as a trickster could have served no other purpose.

The various adventures of Raven or *Yethl* as he is properly known comprise the inspiration for many Tlingit and Haida totem pole carvings. According to one of the many versions of the story, long before the creation of the world, there dwelt in the Land of Supernatural Beings, a powerful chief. He had a beautiful wife of whom he was so jealous that he kept her in a box suspended from the ceiling of his house. Since, according to custom, one of his nephews would inherit her in the event of his death, he was fearful lest they slay him to get her. So to forestall such an eventuality, he killed both his nephews before they became men.

The mother of the slain boys who was the sister of the chief, fled to a lonely spot to mourn her loss. It was there that *Crane* appeared before her, and learning the cause of her grief, instructed her how to replace her loss. She was told to pick a smooth, round pebble from the beach, heat it in the fire and swallow it. She followed Crane's directions and in due time a son was born to her whom she named *Yethl.*

Fearing that he, too, would be killed if her brother heard about him, she concealed the fact of his birth from the Chief. But Yethl was no ordinary son. In ten days he had grown to the full stature of a man and she could no longer conceal him. Presenting him to her brother, she was warmly congratulated and the Chief pretended great friendship for his new nephew. Secretly, however, he planned to do away with him, also.

One day the Chief took Yethl fishing with him, intending to drown him. But when the canoe was capsized, Yethl, who had on his magic diving suit, walked along the bottom until he reached

89

the shore and so returned home unscathed. At another time the murderous Chief tried to trap him in an unfinished canoe but Yethl not only escaped but brought the canoe home.

After repeated attempts to murder his nephew, the Chief gave up and went off hunting, leaving Yethl alone for the first time. As the Chief has suspected, Yethl went immediately to the box holding the beautiful woman and cut it down. But as he lifted her out, two small birds that had been concealed in her armpits, flew up and out through the smoke hole. Knowing that they would warn his uncle, Yethl changed himself into a Raven and flew up into the sky.

Informed by his feathered spies of his nephew's act, the Chief, in great rage, ordered the seas to rise and flood the land, expecting to drown his rival. But Yethl clung to the heavens with his bill and when he could cling no longer, floated down to the sea and landed in a bed of seaweed.

Yethl now ordered *Sea Otter* to dive down and bring up some sand which it did, and out of this sand he created the barren earth. Seaweed, which he chewed up and spat onto the sand, became vegetation of all kinds. He next created fish and animals and finally, man. He tried first to make man out of stone but was not satisfied with his work. Stone was too strong and enduring and he became apprehensive lest the gods should think that man might be too powerful. So, instead, he made man out of wood, and pleased with his success, made woman of wood, also.

Yethl now seems to have taken on the role of man's chief benefactor. He brought fire to the world by carrying a burning brand in his beak from the island where all fire was kept at that time. When the fire burned his beak he dropped the brand and fire was deposited in the sticks and stones wherever

AUKE VILLAGE. Auke Village, about 16 miles northwest of Juneau on Glacier Highway was abandoned shortly after gold was discovered at Juneau in 1880 and the populace moved to the gold camp for work and excitement.

A totem pole and recreation area now mark the village site but none of the old community houses remain.

the sparks fell. Man thereafter could get it out by striking the stones together or rubbing the dry wood *with great vigor.*

He stole fresh water from its owner, Ganook, when he was a guest in his home. But in trying to escape with it by flying out through the smokehole, the spirits of the smokehole held him prisoner long enough to blacken his feathers permanently. Prior to that time Raven had been white but since that incident, all ravens have been black.

As Yethl flew across the earth, drops of water falling from his beak produced lakes and rivers and smaller droplets made the creeks and springs.

Yethl's effort to get light for the world was an adventure that provided material for many totem poles in different styles and versions. According to a Tlingit version, Yethl's world was one of darkness, for another great magician known as *Raven-at-the-head-of-the-Nass* had the sun, moon and stars all boxed up in his house. Yethl intended to steal the sun but the problem was how to get into the closely-guarded house.

From *Frog,* Yethl learned that the magician, who, incidentally is also shown in the sculptures as a raven, had a daughter. *Mink,* the girl's personal servant was inveigled into telling him of a spring where the maiden went daily for a drink of water. By transforming himself into a hemlock needle and dropping into her drinking water, Yethl was accidentally swallowed and in due time was reborn as the magician's grandson. Thus, he gained access into the guarded house.

Young Raven, as Yethl is known at this stage of his adventures, was reborn in human form, but his Raven ancestry was revealed in his sharp, blinking eyes. He succeeded in endearing himself to his unsuspecting grandfather who gratified his every whim. When he cried endlessly for one of the boxes hanging from the ceiling he was finally given it to play with. But as soon as he was left alone he removed the ropes that bound it shut and took off the cover. There were the stars; Yethl was disappointed that the box had not contained the sun. So, after playing marbles with the stars for a while, he tossed them out through the smoke hole where they took their places and remained there.

Since the stars were not bright enough to produce daylight, Yethl began crying again for another of the boxes that hung from the rafters. And at length, his grandfather gave in to his cries and took down the box that contained the moon. As before, Yethl watched his chance and when alone, removed the moon and tossed it out through the smoke hole. It soared up into the heavens and took its place among the stars. But, even casting their light to the earth together, the stars and the moon were not able to change night into day.

Yethl now knew that the remaining box contained the sun and he was determined to get it. He cried so continuously that his grandfather, fearful that the child might die, finally took down his proudest possession and gave it to the child. This time Yethl did not bother to open the box. As soon as he was alone he changed himself back into a Raven and, taking the box, flew out through the smoke hole. As soon as he felt safe from pursuit, he resumed human form and started walking northward looking for people. Eventually he came to a village on the opposite side of a large river. He called to the people, asking them to come and help him across but they would not. Then he told him that he was bringing them daylight but still they would not believe him or help him. Finally, out of patience, Yethl opened the box and a great, blinding light sprang forth. The people were terrified and tried to escape from it. Those who were wearing the skins of animals rushed into the woods and became *Forest People*, the animals we see today. Those having on garments made from the hides of sea animals plunged into the water and became *Sea People*, known today as seals, sealions, whales and fish. Those wearing bird skin clothing flew into the air and became *People of the Sky*. That is why these Indians still regard all of these beings as humans in disguise, but who, on occasion or at home alone, resume human form.

Other Raven stories, possibly of more recent date, indicate that much of Yethl's character was suggested by observation of the bird, itself. Ravens are common throughout the totempolar region and are noted for their voracious appetites, audacity, cunning, humor and sagacity.

The Haidas and Tsimshians also have stories wherein Raven is featured as creator or special benefactor of man. They show evidence of having been borrowed from the Tlingit, and often the details of several of Yethl's adventures are boiled into one story. As one proceeds southward, the Raven stories fade out until, leaving the totem pole area, we find his place taken by other tricksters such as *Coyote*.

Some myths are told for the purpose of explaining or accounting for certain taboos. The story of *Shin-quo-klah* or *Moldy End* is one of such, told in numerous versions by all three Northern tribes to account for the salmon taboos which were observed in the taking, processing, storing, and consumption of salmon, the bread of the land.

CHIEF SHAKES POLE OR "THE WRANGELL RAVEN." Concerning this totem pole, Dr. Thwing, missionary, wrote to the Alaskan (Sitka) Feb. 29, 1896, as follows: "This winter there has been a very general feeling of suspense and expectancy in view of the great feast and intertribal dance for which Chief Shakes has been preparing for a year or two. To dignify a living son, and commemorate one dead, there has been a new totem pole carved, and the Tongass natives have been called to dance and feast here. These guests arrived Feb. 1st, and were received with great honor and much noise."

(Photo by author).

Shin-quo-klah, a high caste Tlingit boy, according to the Haidas, lived at Karta Bay on the east coast of Prince of Wales Island before the Haidas occupied that area. One day, being hungry, he asked his mother for a piece of dried salmon. She gave him some that had been kept two years, something not usually done. Finding the salmon moldy at one end, the boy threw it into the water and then went down to the beach to set snares for seagulls. Some time later, other children playing on the shore discovered a seagull in his snare and called to him. Shin-quo-klah ran down to the beach to remove the bird but it struggled out into deep water and the boy followed. Suddenly, just as he grasped for the gull, he disappeared under the waves. The children who saw what happened, shouted the alarm and the people came down and tried to rescue the boy. They thought he had stepped into a hole and was drowned but though they searched for his body for many days they never found it.

But Shin-quo-klah was not drowned. He had only been pulled beneath the sea by the *Salmon People* who wanted to reward him. For in throwing the moldy salmon into the water, he had given back the life of one of their people. It was only when salmon were eaten and the remains burned or thrown back into the water that Salmon People could resume their life in human form in their villages beneath the sea.

Shin-quo-klah was placed in a large canoe and after several days' travelling, found himself in a village made up of community houses similar to those in which his people resided. But the doors were alive, and the houseposts could talk. He was

shown the Shark House whose entrance was crescent-shaped like a shark's mouth and studded with large, sharp teeth. Bad people lived there, he was told, and he was warned to stay away from them.

In the Salmon People's village, the boy became very hungry but he didn't know how to get any food. Then someone told him if he was hungry he should go the Herring People's house. People would be dancing there, they said, but what appeared to be feathers flying in the air were something else, they said. He was instructed to take a hemlock bough and hold it inside the doorway, keeping his eyes closed. When it got heavy he was to withdraw it and there he'd find something good to eat. Following these instructions, the boy found that the feathers that clung to his hemlock bough were actually herring eggs of which he ate his fill. That is why Indians still spread hemlock boughs on the beach each spring. Then when the herring spawn, at high tide these branches are covered with herring eggs on which they feast.

On another occasion when he was hungry for fish, a woman who was solid stone from the waist down, called him to her side. "If you are hungry," she said, "go down to Amusement Creek where the children are playing. Club one of them as you would a salmon, and you will find something to eat. Amusement Creek got its name from the fact that great flocks of ducks, geese, gulls, cranes and brant played there and made a great noise calling to each other. On a different occasion when he was lonesome and downhearted, they had taken him there to cheer him up and had put his arms around a prancing sandhill crane's neck.

Shin-quo-klah was reluctant to hurt any of the children but finally, the pangs of hunger getting the best of him, he struck one of them with a stick. Instantly it changed into a bright young spring salmon. The boy built a fire and roasted the fish at once. After his meal he threw the remains of the fish into the water and returned to the village feeling much better.

The town was in an uproar when Shin-quo-klah returned. One of the Chief's children had a terrible toothache and they could do nothing for it. The Stone Woman then caught the boy's attention and called him to her. She told him that it must be his fault, and urged him to go back to see if he had thrown all of the bones into the water.

When Shin-quo-klah reached the place where he had cooked the fish he made a careful search. Then he found it! At the bottom of the hole in which he had stuck his roasting stick was part of the salmon's jawbone. This he threw into the water and hurried

HAIDA VILLAGE OF KASA-AN. Kasaan, or *beautiful town* was the seat of Chief Skowl whose house is shown at the right. The stairs between the tall totem poles was a favorite place for tourists of the gay '90's to be photographed. At the time of the Purchase of Alaska, Skowl's son-in-law, Vincent Baronovich was reported "to have a government of his own, and did not recognize the Yankee government."

back to the village. All was peaceful there again. The child's tooth had stopped aching and everybody was happy.

Once when Shin-quo-klah went swimming with some of the Salmon People boys, he leaped above the surface of the water. Nearby was a canoe in which two Indians were sitting. "Look!" shouted one, "There is a bright young spring salmon!" That was the first time that the boy realized that even he now appeared as a salmon to men.

Two or three seasons went by and then one day the Chief told his people to get ready to take a long trip. Hundreds of people poured out of every house and began streaming down to the beach where they boarded huge dugout canoes. Then the canoes were organized into companies, each of which was under the direction of a leader who sat in the bow. Then when all were ready, the great armada started off toward the mouths of the rivers and the villages of men. They were going to fight the battle of the leaves, they said, but Shin-quo-klah didn't understand.

As the army moved along all the people were in high spirits. They met great companies of Herring People returning from a recent trip to the land of men. "Why are you black under your backbones?" twitted the Herring-folk. "Where is your cheek fat?" returned the Salmon. "Our eggs are our cheek fat!" proudly answered the Herring People.

As the mouth of each river or creek was reached, the Salmon Chief assigned a company to enter it. But occasionally a river was passed by, completely. This would be a place where people lived who had disobeyed the salmon taboos and were being punished by starvation.

Shin-quo-klah was in the company dispatched to enter the river beside which stood his native village. As he swam in close to the river bank he found it lined with squatting women, all busily cleaning fish for drying. Among them was the boy's own mother. To these women, the salmon in the pool before them appeared to be *finning* like they always do before they go up the river. But Shin-quo-klah knew that they were actually laughing at the women and he was embarrassed. As he swam in close to admonish his mother to pull down her skirt, she espied him and, calling to her husband said, "Here is a bright young spring salmon. Spear it for our supper."

The salmon was speared and brought home. But when the husband attempted to cut off its head, the knife would not go through. Examining the blade to see what was the matter, the astonished man saw on its edge, little fragments of copper.

TAGCOOK'S TOTEM POLE. This 65″ pole was carved for Wrangell businessmen by Charlie Tagcook, professional Chilkat totem carver, and dedicated during the Wrangell Potlatch in 1940. It tells three stories, "How Raven got Light for the World" and the "Jonah" story. The bottom figure is Goo-teekhl, the Cannibal Giant and the small white face on his chest is "Mosquito." They recall the famous Chilkat story on the "Origin of Mosquitos."

(Photo by the author).

93

ELDERLY HAIDAS AND HEIRLOOMS. The decorated bentwood tray in the center is made of yew wood, probably from the Queen Charlotte Islands, although the yew grows sparsely to a little north of Ketchikan. Trays like these were so highly regarded by the Haidas that they were protected from profane eyes as well as the elements by woven cedarbark slip covers. The appliqued blanket design represents the North Wind.

Photo by the author.

Suddenly he remembered that his lost son was wearing a copper collar when he disappeared.

Realizing that he was dealing with the supernatural and that everything would depend on his actions, he first ordered all the women out of his household so that there could be nothing unclean that might offend the spirits. Then all the men were ordered to drink salt water in order to purify themselves for the undertaking that was to follow.

When all was in readiness, the salmon was placed in a new basket and set under the roof in a place where the eaves would drip on it. Slowly the skin parted and began to slip away. Little by little, the miniature form of their lost son began to appear. Finally, the skin fell away completely revealing the boy as he was when he was lost except that he was only about two feet long. Once restored to his home, the boy grew rapidly and in a few days was restored to his former size.

From that day on, Shin-quo-klah, because of his experience with the super natural, was wise beyond his years and as he grew into manhood became a great Shaman. He taught the people the salmon taboos and saw to it that they were never broken. The result was that the people along the Karta River always lived in abundance.

Many years went by and the Shaman became very old. In fact, Shin-quo-klah lived far longer than anyone had ever lived before. His hair which had never been cut nearly reached to the ground. He was greatly respected by everyone because of his great wisdom and venerable years.

One summer day the river was full of spawning salmon and as usual all of the villagers were at work putting up their winter's supply. Then one of them chanced to see a salmon that was different from any they had ever seen before. It seemed to be transparent like glass and in some accounts it was said to have had a red feather in its head, worn like a plume. At once a band of men and boys assembled on the river bank and tried to spear it. But try as they did, not one of them could hit it. Noticing the excitement, old Shin-quo-klah hobbled down to the river bank to see what was going on.

Someone handed him a spear, saying, "Here, see if you can hit it. None of us can." The old Shaman took the spear reluctantly, aimed and hurled it. It went straight to the mark, struck the salmon in the neck, killing it. But at the same instant, Shin-quo-klah fell to the ground, dying. The supernatural salmon was his own soul and he had killed it.

Before he died, Shin-quo-klah made his last request. He asked that he be dressed in his Shaman's robes and that he and all his paraphrenalia be placed on a raft and floated down the river. This request was carried out and the raft bearing the dead Shaman and his drums was set adrift. Down the river it went straight as an arrow until it came opposite a steep cliff. There the raft spun around in a whirlpool four times and sank.

Indians say that even today when important things are about to happen to those Karta River people, Shin-quo-klah's drum can be heard from the depths, beating a muffled warning. And some say he still comes up the river each spawning season with the salmon. One old man who has seen him says he is only about four feet long but his hair trails many feet behind him.

The legends of these totem carvers are principally made up of tales of migrations, the flood, intertribal wars, and early contacts with white men. All groups have accounts of a flood that inundated all of the land save the highest peaks. Curiously, these accounts are so localized that the major mountain peak in any locality is generally referred to as the one on which the people were saved by one means

CHIEF SHAKES VI (Gush-klin II) SEATED AMONG HIS TREASURES. With the exception of the house pillars, all property shown here has since been dispursed. The principal clan symbols of the Wrangell *Nan-yaa-yi* as here displayed, are Grisly Bear, Dogfish Shark, Killer Whale. The creature in the center with long ears and fins is the *Gonakadate*, a mythological sea monster that is probably the personified *Whirlpool*. The antlered headdress on the chest at the rear represents *Gowakan*, or Deer and is worn by a peace emissary or on ceremonial occasions in the Peace Dance. On the right rear wall can be seen the famous *Shakes* Chief's staff or sceptre surmounted by the *Killerwhale*. The house pillars came from *Kutku Hit* or *Shark House*, an earlier community house at Kotslitan, some 18 miles south of Wrangell. That town was abandoned after 1833-34 when the Russians built Redoubt St. Dionysius at the present site of Wrangell, the exact location of which is known.

INDIAN SALESWOMAN. Fifty years ago, passengers on tourist cruise ships visiting Southeastern Alaska found the docks lined with Indian women selling spruceroot baskets, berries, model totem poles, horn spoons, moccasins, and various carvings. A few still survive but their stock is mostly of beaded sealskin moccasins.

In this studio photo the saleswoman bears a *button blanket,* a beaded headdress, several strings of trade beads and a silver nose ring. The cane in her hands is no doubt a replica of an early *chief's staff,* a symbol of authority. A number of clues such as the moosehide mocassins, the Chilkat blanket-like woven piece at the throat and the style of the carving at the left, label the woman, *Chilkat.*

or another. The story is the inspiration for several totem poles, notably the Bear totem mortuary pole of the Nanyaayi at Wrangell and the Devil's Thumb pole of the same place.

The Haidas have legends of migrations from the East Coast of the Queen Charlotte Islands to the West Coast and from North Island (Langara) across Dixon's Entrance to Dall Island in Alaska. Both of these legends are historically correct, the migrations having occurred within the past two hundred and fifty years or so. They have no legends telling of any earlier homeland although they generally believe that they come from a distant land to the south. As proof they cite the fact that they were obliged to adopt Tlingit names for things in their new environment that were not present in the old.

Tlingit migration stories tell of crossing great continental plains and mountain ranges but do not mention crossing seas. At one place in their great trek, three-bladed grass cut their legs like knives and the injured had to be sent back to the rear. Following a great river to the coast, they found their descent to the sea cut off by a glacier that bridged the river. Strong young men went over the glacier to view the country beyond. But old men, soon to die anyway, went under the glacier to see if it were possible to get through alive. When they emerged safe the news was carried back to the migrating tribe and the main body passed under the obstructing glacier. This feat gave rise to a Tlingit axiom to the effect that "when difficulties are too great to be surmounted, go under them."

Arriving at the coast, the Tlingit expanded northward and were already in the Prince William Sound country attacking the Eskimos there when the Russians arrived. It is generally agreed that they formerly lived in the region now occupied by the Tsimshian but it is not established that they were pushed out by them. Some Tlingit families even claim origin in the Queen Charlotte Islands but it is not known that the Haidas displaced them there either.

The story of the migrations of the Nan-yaa-yi clan of Wrangell is typical of many of the Tlingit legends. A large band of Indians of the Wolf totem

96

descended the Taku river and established itself nearby at Taku Inlet. From this band as time went on, groups migrated to other more favorable locations. One such band built a community house at Hoonah but was burned out. From the charred main timbers they constructed a new house, thereby acquiring the clan name *Kok-wan-ton* or *People-who-live-under-burned-timbers*. Two other groups turned southward and eventually ascended the Stikine river. One band settled at the *signa* or *grindstone* place and came to be known as the *Signahudi*. The other group went to a place *beyond* and thereby acquired the name *Nan-yaa-yi* or *the-people-camped-beyond*. There they became wealthy in trade since their location made them the middlemen between the interior *Tahltan* and *Kaska* and the coast people. These interior Indians came in time to regard the Nan-yaa-yi chiefs as their overlords.

As time went on some of the Nan-yaa-yi returned to the mouth of the Stikine river and resided on an island there for several generations. But the bitter Stikine wind finally drove them out and they built a new town a few miles to the south, called *Chugas-an*, or waterfall town. Here inter-tribal trouble caused another split-up, and one chief and his followers moved away. On Wrangell island, at a point some twenty-five miles away, a stand of willows was seen and regarded as a good omen for it reminded the migrants of the river country where they had once lived. Here they built a new town known as *Kotslit-an*, or Willow Town. Today its ruins are known as *Old Wrangell*.

There came a time of warfare with the Nass river Tsimshian but the Nan-yaa-yi were finally victorious and their chief acquired the Tsimshian chief's name, *We-shakes*, which was subsequently shortened to *Shakes*. This began a succession of chiefs who inherited the name, the seventh of which died in 1944. It was the fourth chief of this line, *Shaut-shugo-ish* who abandoned Kotslit-an and led his people to Wrangell, eighteen miles to the north where they built a new village under the guns of the Russian fort which was completed there in 1834.

The best-known Chief Shakes was *Kow-ish-te* (Shakes V), the nephew of Shaut-shugo-ish. During his chieftainship, Redoubt St. Dionysius, the Russian fort at Wrangell, was leased to the British and in 1840, the name of the station was changed to *Fort Stikine*. He was still the Chief in 1867 when the Americans took over and the village came to be known to the American military as *Fort Wrangell*, subsequently altered to Wrangell. From then on the Indian legends merge with American history, and Indian affairs are fairly-well documented thereafter.

Many Indian legends tell of the natives' first encounters with white men and the Haida actually celebrated their discovery of Victoria, B.C. and made a button blanket to commemorate the event.

Although there seem to be no accounts of the landings of Chirikof and Bering in 1741, there are accounts of La Perouse at Lituya Bay and Captain George Vancouver at several points. Mackenzie who reached the coast after an overland journey in 1793 found Coast Indians who had seen Vancouver and Menzies, referring to them as *Macubah* and *Ben-zins*.

THE BEAVER TOTEM POLE. Shown here in front of the *Flying Raven House* in Wrangell, this pole was sold then taken down and sectioned for storage. The beaver on top was too rotted for salvage but the other three segments finally were purchased by the State Museum and may now be seen there. Four stories are here recalled: that of the Killisnoo Beaver, The man who destroyed the Giant Octopus, Duk-toothl, the strong man, shown here rending a sea lion apart, and Kayak, a hero seen here strangling a sea monster.

Photo by F. W. Carylon.

CEREMONIAL OIL BOWLS. Types of ceremonial oil bowls of mountain sheep horn and wood popular on the Northwest Coast but made principally by Haida and Tsimshian. Hawks, beavers, bears and killerwhales and some supernatural beings were the principal motifs.

Photo by the author from a plate in the Berlin Museum for Volkerkunde portfolio, "The Northwest Coast of America" 1883.

A Tsimshian story of their first encounter with white men concerns one *Sabahan* who was some distance offshore fishing for halibut when his party saw a strange monster approaching them out of the fog. It was black and shiny, and its numerous long legs lifted then touched the water with rhythmic beat, causing it to move over the water at an astonishing speed. Sabahan and his companions pulled up their lines and started for shore, paddling furiously. But the monster took after them, gaining at every stroke. Sabahan, believing they would all be killed, tied his kelp fishline around his body and fastened it to the canoe, hoping thereby that his body would at least be found. But the canoe reached shore first and the Indians sprang out, disappearing in the forest. That is, all except poor Sabahan. He had forgotten that he had tied himself to the canoe. He ran until, coming to the end of the line, he was suddenly snapped back into the arms of his pursuers. As it turned out, it was not a water monster, after all. It was only a band of friendly men with pale faces, dressed in dripping black oilskins.

Using sign language, the white men indicated that they wanted Sabahan to build a fire. He understood them, and taking some wax out of his ear, and some equipment out of the boat, started to make fire by friction. The white men, apparently believing this ancient process too tedious, gathered some dry grass. Then one of them, taking a pistol from his belt, fired into the heap of grass. Immediately it burst into flame but the loud report of the pistol caused Sabahan to fall to the ground in a faint. When he came to, he felt himself all over carefully to see where he had been hurt but found he was whole. Then, believing that he was in the presence of supernatural beings who were dealing in magic, Sabahan urinated into his hands, then washed his face in it, this being the approved preventative of witchcraft.

Presently the white men, indicating the halibut in

98

Sabahan's canoe, made known through signs that they wanted him to prepare some for cooking. Sabahan began dressing the fish with a mussel shell but was soon stopped. Then one of the men pulled something bright and shining from his side, struck the fish a few rapid blows and it fell in pieces before the amazed eyes of Sabahan.

The other Indians who had been lurking in the trees, watching, were now beckoned by Sabahan to come out of hiding since he was sure the strange men meant no harm. Sometime later the white men were guided to the village where the fishermen lived and were feasted on Indian food and given presents. Then the Indians were invited out to Vancouver's ship to taste white men's food and to receive a return of presents.

As they approached the ship riding at anchor, its sails furled, the Indians became very uneasy. The rigging of the ship looked like the web of a gigantic spider and the blocks appeared to them as the heads of its victims. But Sabahan reassured them and the visiting party went aboard.

First they were offered pilot bread or hardtack but it looked to them like the bracket fungi or conks that grow on dead trees. Sabahan tasted it first and finding it good, recommended it to his friends. Then they were offered boiled rice but it looked to them like white maggots. Again Sabahan tasted it and pronounced it good, whereupon the others fell to. Then they were offered molasses to eat on their rice. This they refused, believing it to be spoiled blood, but Sabahan tasted it warily and pronounced it sweet. After that they all ate heartily and enjoyed the new food.

Presents were then distributed to all. Some were given knives, others hatchets, beads, buttons, small bells and articles of clothing. But Sabahan received the most wonderful gift of all. It was a small mirror

TRAYS AND BOWLS. Various types of trays and bowls once common on the Northwest Coast. All displayed here are *dugout* except the tray in the upper left hand corner which is of *bentwood* construction. Trays were usually of yew but some of them and all of the wooden bowls were made of alder which imparted no scent or taste to the food or oil. Bowls made for serving seal oil were often carved in a stylized seal design such as those shown here. The receptacle in the center is Kwakiutl but Haida, Tsimshian or Tlingit could have made the dugout trays and seal bowls.

Photo by the author from a plate in the Berlin Museum for Volkerkunde portfolio, "The Northwest Coast of America" 1883.

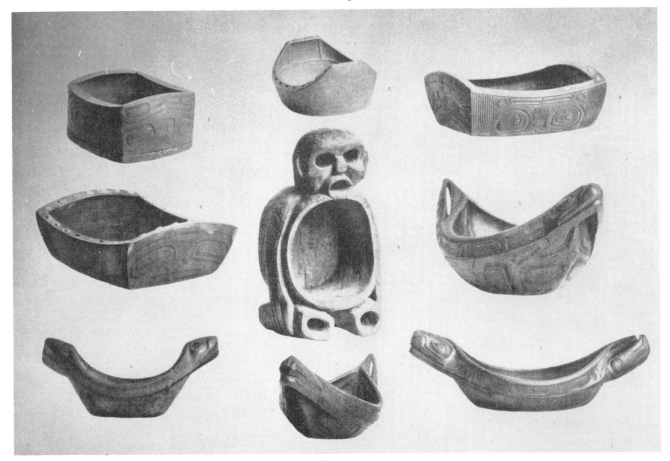

KWAKIUTL ART. Exampes of Kwakiutl art. The carvings at the lower left and right appear to be remnants of an earlier local art style that gave way to the conventionalized art imported from the Tsimshian and Haida to the north. Similar remnants of an earlier Tlingit art have been collected.

Photo by the author from a plate in the Berlin Museum for Volkerkunde portfolio, "The Northwest Coast of America" 1883.

in which he saw his own face for the first time. With this mirror, Sabahan became a very wealthy man. People came to believe that in it they could see their future. And Sabahan, capitalizing on their credulity, charged them so much a look.

Numerous tales, sometimes tragic, often humorous, recount the receiving of firearms for the first time. According to one of them, a group of Haidas, having purchased their first musket, got into an argument concerning the proper method of aiming. One said that white men held it to the shoulder. Another one insisted that it must be held against the nose so you could look down the barrel with both eyes. He won the argument and the right to demonstrate the method, getting a broken nose for his pains.

One chief had great fun with his new musket shooting other Indians off a cliff. The spectators thought it was great fun until they discovered to their great surprise that their friends were being killed. On another occasion, a war flotilla of Haidas met a similar warring party of Tsimshians and moved in for battle. The Haidas had a musket which they suddenly fired into the air. The amazed Tsimshians leaped into the water and the battle was over.

Traders on the Coast who first sold muskets to the natives, withheld powder and shot from the unsuspecting Indians. One old man brought his gun back for a trade-in, exclaiming, "Whatsa-matter him allatime go *click,* no go *Pow!*" Still afraid to trust the natives with firearms, they sold them powder but no shot. It was not long, however, until the

100

Indians were melting up pewter pots for shot and even firing charges of gold and copper nuggets in lieu of lead.

There are Indian accounts of the battle of Sitka between Tlingit and Russian under Baranof but according to their accounts, the Indians won the battle. The story of the bombardment and burning of Kake village in 1869 by the gunboat Saginaw as told by Kake natives is surprisingly similar to published accounts. But the story of the Kake Indians killing Colonel Ebey on Whidbey Island in 1857 in an act of reprisal, and carrying off his head as a trophy seems to have been forgotten entirely.

Indians of the totempolar regions still like to tell stories and reminisce on the old times but with the passing of the community house, story-telling gatherings are few and far between. The general adoption of the English language and the coming of schools and churches have contributed to the extinction of native literature. Few of the young people today know any of their own stories and almost none can tell the significance of totem poles. But sometimes, out on hunting, fishing or trapping trips, sitting around camp fires, the old spirit returns and Raven is again Yethl. Then the woods are filled with supernatural beings, animals are again people, and witches are rampant. Then, and only then, the gray-haired natives can be induced to tell a story such as their grandparents told them in the days before white men came.

MASKS. Masks were worn in theatricals and by shamans during their incantations. Human hair was often used to decorate ceremonial objects, particularly by the Tlingit, but the cannibal bird at the upper left has hair of shredded cedar bark. It is a Kwakiutl manufacture.

Photo by the author from a plate in the Berlin Museum for Volkerkunde portfolio, "The Northwest Coast of America" 1883.

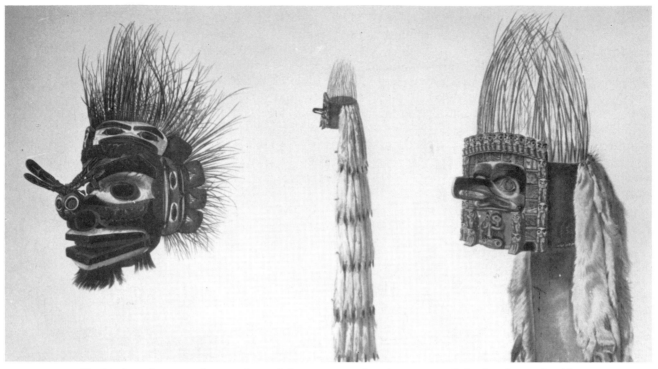

MASKS. Kwakiutl masks were often mechanical, being operated with strings, and displayed considerable genius. A departure from traditional Northwest Coast art style is to be seen in the geometrical designs on the whale's dorsal fin.

SHAMAN'S OUTFIT. The object at center above is a *soul catcher* used by the shaman to trap and return a wandering soul to its owner. In the center is a woven spruce root hat. The other objects are rattles, a clapper and a charm, also part of a shaman's outfit, although rattles were used by dancers as well.

Photos by the author from a plate in the Berlin Museum for Volkerkunde portfolio, "The Northwest Coast of America" 1883.

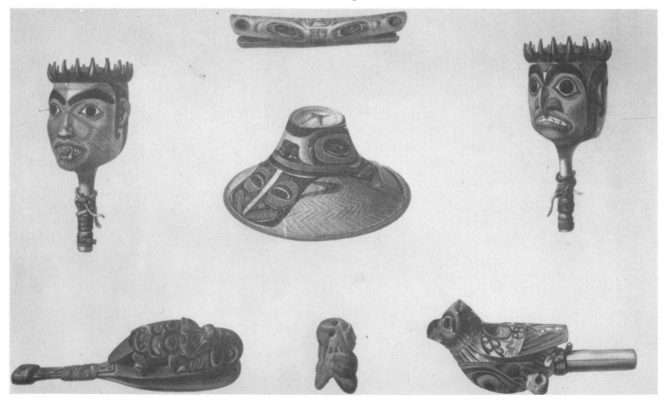

Chapter Ten

THE POTLATCH

No book on the subject of totem poles would be complete without some discussion of the much-libeled *Potlatch,* for on the Northwest Coast the two are often closely related, especially with the Haida. So far as the Tlingit are concerned, the Potlatch was a religious ceremony, the motive underlying it being respect for the dead, as well as an opportunity to reward those of the opposite phratry who had assisted at a burial. The erecting of a totem pole by the Tlingit on these occasions did not necessarily follow, especially in the northern part of their domain. However, if a pole was raised it would be a memorial to the dead, and not a Potlatch pole such as the Haidas erected.

The true Potlatch of the Haida was given by a Chief to members of his own phratry. It was purely social and intended to build up his reputation and increase his social standing. The elaborate pole erected of this occasion stood as a witness and a validation of what had taken place.

There were numerous ceremonies held by the various Indian peoples of the Northwest Coast and each had its especial function and individual name. White man has seldom taken the trouble to examine the institutions of the primitive people with whom he comes in contact, and as a result often misunderstands and confuses one with the other. All ceremonies held by the Indians on the Coast were regarded as Potlaches by the whites and were generally regarded as *bad medicine.* Missionaries notably could see nothing in them but wasteful barbarous orgies and set about to end them by one means or another.

It was in defending this Indian institution that the later Doctor Franz Boas, father of American anthropology, writing in the Victoria Province under date of Feb. 11, 1897 defined the Potlatch so aptly:

"The economic system of the Indians of British Columbia and Alaska is largely based on credit, just as much as that of civilized communities. In all of his undertakings the Indian relies on the help of his friends. He promises to pay them for this help at a later date. If the help furnished consisted in valuables—which are measured by the Indians by blankets as we measure them by money—he promises to repay the amount so loaned with interest. The Indian has no system of writing and, therefore, in order to give security to the transaction it is performed publicly. The contracting of debts on the one hand and the paying of debts on the other is the potlatch. This economic system has developed to such an extent that the capital possessed by all the individuals of the tribe combined exceeds many times the actual amount of cash that exists. That is to say the conditions are quite analogous to those prevailing in our community: if we want to call in all

POTLATCH GUESTS ARRIVE. Kake Indians, guests of Chief Shakes at his 1940 Wrangell Potlatch arrive by dugout war canoe as in the days before white men and their gasboats. This is the famous Killerwhale canoe that was lost in the Wrangell fire of 1952. The Potlatch was held at the instance of the U.S. Forest Service to commemorate restoration of the Chief Shakes Community House and totem poles on Shakes Island in Wrangells' inner harbor. By adopting the Wrangell Chamber of Commerce into his clan, Shakes obtained the financing to hold the last big potlatch at which he assumed the authentic title of Shakes VII.

our outstanding debts, it is found that there is not, by any means, money enough in existence to pay them, and the result of an attempt of all the creditors to call in their loans results in disastrous panic from which it takes the community a long time to recover.

"It must be clearly understood that an Indian who invites all his friends and neighbors to a great potlatch, and apparently squanders all the accumulated results of long years of labor, has two things in his mind which we cannot but acknowledge as wise and worthy of praise. His first object is to pay his debts. This is done publicly and with much ceremony, as a matter of record. His second object is to invest the fruits of his labor so that the greatest benefit will accrue from them for his own benefit as well as for his children. The recipients of gifts at this festival receive these as loans, which they utilize in their present undertakings. But after the lapse of several years they must repay them with interest to the giver or to his heir. Thus the potlatch comes to be considered by the Indians as a means of insuring the well-being of their children if they should be left orphans while still young; it is, we might say, his life insurance.

"The sudden abolition of this system, which in all its intricacies is very difficult to understand, but the main points of which are set forth in the preceding remarks, destroys all the accumulated capital of the Indians. It undoes the carefully planned life-work of the present generations, exposes them to need in their old age, and leaves the orphans unprovided. What wonder, that it is resisted with

vigour by the best class of Indians, and that only the lazy ones support it because it relieves them of the duty to pay their debts.

"But it will be said, that cruel ceremonies connected with some of the festivals make their discontinuance necessary. From an intimate knowledge of the Indian character and of these very ceremonies I consider any interference with them unadvisable. They are so intimately connected with all that is sacred to the Indian that their forced discontinuance will tend to destroy what moral steadiness is left to him. It was during these ceremonies that I heard the old men of the tribe exhort the young to mend their ways, that they held up to shame the young women who had gone to Victoria to lead a life of shame and that they earnestly discussed the question of requesting the Indian agents to help them in their endeavor to bring the young back to the good moral life of old.

"And the cruelty of the ceremonial exists alone in the fancy of those who know of it only by the exaggerated descriptions of travelers. In olden times it was a war ceremony and captives were killed and even devoured. But with the encroachment of civilization the horrors of the old ceremony have died out. I heard an old chief addressing his people thus: 'How lovely is our time. No longer do we go in fear of each other. Peace is everywhere. No longer is there the strife of battle; we only try to out do each other in the potlatch,' meaning that each tries to invest his property in the most profitable manner, and particularly that they vie with each other in honorably repaying their debts.

"The ceremony of the present day is no more and no less than a time of general amusement which is expected with much pleasure by young and old. But enough of its old sacredness remains to give the Indian, during the time of its celebration, an aspect of dignity which he lacks at other times. The lingering survivals of the old ceremonies will die out quickly, and the remainder is a harmless amusement that we should be slow to take away from the native who is struggling against the overpowerful influence of civilization."

But for all his scholarship and eloquent pleas on behalf of the native peoples, Boas was only wasting his breath. The first Canadian Indian Act which was enacted in 1880 (Statutes of Canada, 43rd Victoria, Chapter 28) made no mention of potlatches. But in a revision made in 1884 (Stat.Can., 47th Victoria, Ch. 27,Sec. 3) the potlatch was made illegal, and this section became Section 114 of the Indian Act in the Revised Statutes of Canada, 1886 (Ch. 43). The section was revised again to define it more clearly in 1895 (58-59 Vict., Ch. 35, Sec. 6). This became the law which remained in force until 1951. For example, it was Sec. 140 of Ch. 98 of the Revised Statutes of Canada of 1927 which reads as follows: 1. Every Indian or other person who engages in, or assists in celebrating or encourages either directly or indirectly another to celebrate any Indian festival, dance or other ceremony of which the giving away or paying or giving back of money, goods or articles of any sort forms a part, or is a feature, whether such gift of money, goods or articles takes place before, at, or after the celebration of the same, or who engages or assists in any celebration or dance of which the wounding or mutilation of the dead or living body of any human being or animal forms a part or is a feature, is guilty of an offense and is liable on summary conviction to imprisonment for a term not exceeding six months and not less than two months. 2. Nothing in this section shall be construed to prevent the holding of any agricultural show or exhibition or the giving of prizes for exhibits thereat. 3. Any Indian in the province of Manitoba, Saskatchewan, Alberta, or British Columbia, or in the Territories who participate in any Indian dance outside the bounds of his own reserve, or who participates in any show, exhibition, performance, stampede or pageant in aboriginal costume without the consent of the Superintendent General or his authorized agent, and any person who induces or employs any Indian to take part in such dance, show, exhibition, performance, stampede or pageant, or induces any Indian to leave his reserve or employs any Indian for such a purpose, whether the dance, show, ex-

hibition, stampede or pageant has taken place or not, shall on summary conviction be liable to a penalty not exceeding twenty-five dollars, or to imprisonment for one month, or to both penalty and imprisonment. (R.A. C.81. sec.119; 1914,c.35, s.8 1918, c.26.s.7.)

In 1951 a new Indian Act was drawn up which is now in force, and makes no mention of potlatches (15 George VI, Ch. 29.)

Outwardly the Potlatch followed quite a uniform pattern along the entire coast. Preparations went on for several years in which time vast stores of food were gathered and blankets or other articles intended as gifts were collected. Among the Haida the success of the proposed Potlatch was assured by an investigation committee who looked over the food supply as well as the proposed gifts and not until they had voiced approval could the aspiring chief send out his invitations.

If the guests came from a distance they did not go immediately to the appointed place but landed their canoes nearby where faces were painted in the approved manner and festive attire put on. Then, when all was in readiness, they made a ceremonial arrival, singing a peace song from their canoes. This song was answered by the host and his clan who stood before the house which invariably faced the beach. When the visitors had landed they went into an appropriate dance in front of the host after which the entertaining chief gave his welcoming dance. All were then ushered within and seated in opposing groups, according to rank. Feasting followed and there were many speeches by the host or his appointed orators, wherein he was glorified and his rivals scorned and belittled.

Presents were distributed each day, according to

POTLATCH BOWL. On auspicious occasions, the Indians of the Northwest Coast served their honored guests in great style. This is a Haida sheephorn bowl for the individual serving of eulachon grease, the dip of the day. The motif is the stylized blue hawk. Author's collection.

Photo by the author.

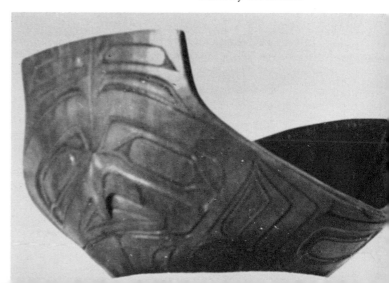

the rank of the recipients. Since wealth and rank were practically synonymous, those of high degree received the most costly presents. It was deemed an insult to give too little and an invitation to trouble to give too much. The reason for this was obvious. Each gift had a string to it, that is, it could not be refused and within a reasonable time it had to be returned with interest else the recipient was disgraced and took a social fall. To give too little implied that the host underestimated his guest's ability to repay and would cause deep resentment. But if he wanted to down a social rival he would purposely give more than the recipient could ever repay. This was a dangerous procedure for the guest might risk a bloody feud with his rival rather than fall beneath him socially.

To ascertain the financial status of each of his proposed guests, the host might employ scouts to spy out information that would aid him in achieving the desired results from the Potlatch. For as Boas has said, the Potlatch was the Haida's system of banking and social security. Judicious gift-giving meant a handsome financial return in due time and would insure the independence of the host in his declining years, or of his children should he not live to receive the returns himself.

The word, *potlatch*, comes from the Chinook *patshatl* via the Chinook jargon and means *giving* or a *gift*. The institution as we know it is believed to be Qwakiutl in origin, spreading north and south along the coast for a thousand miles or so, and even into the interior. However, it is a different sort of *giving* even when no ceremony is involved. For example, if a man has two canoes and his Indian friend has none, the Indian might casually remark that no man needs two canoes, or that he has no canoe, or needs one, or any other of a number of subtle and not too subtle hints. When he has come to believe that the canoe owner is sufficiently impressed of his desires or needs, he potlatches his friend something that he believes is equal in value to the desired canoe. Then, if within a reasonable time the canoe is not forthcoming, he takes back his *gift*, and the deal is off. White men, not understanding this procedure have coined the term *Indian-giver* for anyone who takes back a gift.

About thirty years ago, a band of Canadian Haidas, visiting their Alaskan cousins in a village across the line, distributed gifts throughout the village upon their arrival. However, on the day of their departure all such gifts were gathered up from each house where they had not been "wined, dined, and variously entertained" on potlatch scale.

Payment for services rendered was made at pot-latch-like ceremonies, only here the gift had no strings attached, for a man in this instance was only paying current debts. These debts might represent wages due for assistance in building a house, and would be discharged at a *house-drying-out* ceremony comparable to our own *house-warming*. Or they might have been incurred as the result of a funeral wherein the opposite phratry does all the work.

Great ceremonies or Potlatches were held by the Nootka when they presented their daughters to society; by the Qwakiutl when they purchased or sold a chief's copper, or at the naming of a child, piercing the lip for a labret or any other ceremony that had to be witnessed publicly.

At a funeral, gifts were made to the singers who by their songs helped assuage the grief of the bereaved and lighted the path of the dead. But none of these were true potlatches in that the gift was merely payment and did not have to be returned.

The true Potlatch as a native institution in Southeastern Alaska died at the turn of the century. However, it is not entirely forgotten and many of the older inhabitants still recognize Potlatch obligations. An interesting revival occurred at Wrangell in 1940. The community house and totem poles on Shakes Island had just been restored by the U.S. Forest Service and plans were being made for appropriate dedication ceremonies. It was then that *Kudanake*, the legal successor of the Chief Shakes who died in 1916 expressed the desire to assume the name and position to which he was entitled but had earlier relinquished. And so, to help Kudanake, better known as Charlie Jones, achieve his ambition, the idea of the Wrangell Potlatch was conceived.

In order that the local Chamber of Commerce might aid financially, the entire membership of the organization was adopted into the Nanyaayi clan by Kudanake and several thousand dollars were made available to him to finance the festivity. Tlingits from Kake village were especially invited to dance opposite the chief's clan and confederates. Other invitations went out to unofficial guests or "spectators," several hundred of whom, white and Indian, came from other towns of the Panhandle and from stateside. The Potlatch was colorful and realistic even to those who could not speak the Tlingit tongue in which the songs were sung and the speeches were given. But, entirely unbeknown to the white spectators, during the Potlatch two young Indians, a boy and girl of high caste, received honorary names and Kudanake assumed the traditional title of Chief Shakes, he being the seventh in line to bear that proud name.

Chapter Eleven

CARVING AND ERECTING THE TOTEM POLE

Totem poles and all of their legitimate relatives erected on the Northwest Coast by the totem pole carving Indians were carved of Western red cedar, *thuja plicata*. This tree is not to be confused with Alaska yellow cedar, *chamaecyparis nootkatensis*, which as the name implies is more of the cypress order. Together, these cedars comprise about five percent of the Totemland forests. Alaska cedar, while not used by the Indians for totem poles, is the principal wood used in the carving of model poles. It is a beautiful, fine-grained wood, harder and denser than red cedar and might be compared to white pine as a carving wood. Red cedar, on the other hand, is lighter in weight, softer, and has a tendency to splinter. While not much used for small carvings it was the best wood in the country for dugout canoes, house timbers and totem poles. Alder, which grows throughout the entire area, was used primarily for food dishes and oil bowls since it imparts no odor or flavor to the food. Maple was used for rattles and spoons; crabapple for staffs, canes and mallets. Yew was used for bows and also in the decorative part of wooden halibut hooks. Where red cedar was not available, Sitka spruce was used in house construction and, together with Western hemlock, was a principal fuel. On the coast, driftwood hemlock was preferred for smoking fish, it being nonresinous, but up the rivers alder and cottonwood were used for smoking salmon and served for other purposes as well.

Red cedar does not grow north of 57 degrees N. latitude, running out in the vicinity of Wrangell and Sitka. Yellow cedar is found as far north as Prince William Sound but even at Katalla the house pillars were made of imported red cedar. At Klukwan, on the Chilkat River, canoes are made of cottonwood in lieu of cedar and houses of spruce but all of their house pillars are of imported red cedar as were their war canoes.

In the Queen Charlotte Islands are found the finest of these gigantic cedars, and there were carved the finest totem poles, the best remaining examples of which have been transported to various Canadian cities and set up in their city parks and museums.

When the occasion arose among the Haida for the carving of one of these huge monuments a search was made for a suitable tree as near to the beach as possible. When selected and approved by the chief for whom it was to be carved it was felled, cut to the proper length, trimmed and peeled. Then the side containing the most knots was hollowed out as if in preparing to make a canoe. This hollowing has a dual purpose. First, it reduced the weight, making it easier to skid down to the beach, and lighter when the finished pole was to be erected. But most important, the

107

A NEW TOTEM POLE. Being floated to the place where it is to be erected. The Haidas say that their inspiration for these quaint monuments came from a waterlogged totem pole that drifted to their beaches in the Queen Charlotte Islands from parts unknown many generations ago.

Photo by author.

removal of the heartwood made the pole more resistant to checking. The pole, ready for carving, was a half-round shell, some ten inches thick.

With the preliminary shaping already accomplished in the woods, the log would then be skidded to the beach then towed to the village and beached at the place where the carving was to be done. A professional carver now took over and together with his helpers or slaves, adzed it into shape and then marked it into sections of equal length. Thus a thirty foot pole would contain five sections of six foot length. The Haida paid for the carving by the section and sometimes a different carver was employed for each section. For each of these divisions the equivalent of about $50.00 was paid in blankets.

The carver as an *artist* had little if any personal liberty in his work, his contribution being skill and dexterity and a knowledge of the traditional style. He was told exactly what was to be carved on the monument and traditional style handed down in the form of chief's staffs, horn spoon handles, and later, argillite carvings, dictated the style and manner in which the conventionalized figures would appear in the sculpture. Moreover, a committee of inspectors representing the chief for whom the work was being done had to approve each suggested pattern before the figure was roughed in. Often in the course of carving an important pole, distinguished guests of the chief would be invited to take the adze and make a few token strokes. This was considered a great honor and privilege, comparable to the laying of a cornerstone of a fine public building or driving the first or last spike of an important railroad.

The principal tools used by the totem carver were an assortment of steel hand adzes patterned after earlier adzes that had nephrite jade bits, several knives with curved blades resembling farriers' knives but more likely a bloodbrother of the Eskimo's *mitlik*, or thumb knife. Then there was an assortment of accessory tools and materials such as chisels, mallets of crabapple wood, patterns of sealskin and birchbark, dogfish sharkskin for sanding, plus painting materials and brushes.

Carving began at the top or upper end over which a portable shelter or tent was sometimes erected to shelter the artisan from inclement weather. As the work progressed down the pole the shelter was advanced accordingly. After the pole had been adzed down to its contemplated size, general shape and taper, and the sections laid out, patterns for the figures were laid on for the first or upper figure, and outlined. Patterns were not used for all parts, freehand drawing serving in their stead. But in the carving of an eye, separate patterns were used for the eyeball, the opening outline, and the bean-shaped carving that represented the eye socket. This procedure was necessary to assure that the eyes match each other in size and shape. A late refinement was that of a taut string drawn from the center of the base to the top center to keep the figures in proper balance and alignment but the lack of this innovation can be seen in a number of poles.

Mandibles, fins etc. that stood out at right angles to the pole were mortized in before carving. A rectangular aperture was first chiseled out, into which a block of cedar of suitable size was driven in by maul or mallet. Where glueing was necessary, glue was made by boiling down halibut fins. Carving of the beak or fin was done after the rough block had been mortized in, and the block being oversize, became part of the face or back as the case might be. This greatly strengthened these parts causing them to last much longer than they would have, had they been doweled in after completion. Wings were made separately unless folded, being attached with wooden dowels.

Much of the beauty of Northwest Coast sculpture was due to the *hammer-track* finish put on over the entire surface of the carving. This was accomplished by means of a small adze, not over an inch across the blade which was rounded at the edge and slightly concave. A skillful carver could go over the surface of any totem carving, taking off uniform chips about the size of a dime, achieving an indented surface similar to that produced on copper by pein-hammering. The quality of this texturing often was the deciding factor between good and mediocre carving.

The Haida did not hollow out their house pillars since they had to bear a heavy load and hollowing would weaken them. Many of the totem poles were so slender that it was both impractical and unnecessary to hollow or even flatten them at the rear. Others, such as the *Wolf-tail* pole that formerly stood at Sukkwan would have lost its realism had it not been left *in the round*.

With the exception of their house pillars, the Tlingit rarely hollowed out their cedar monuments. The smaller ones were left round or squared, while others were flattened or very slightly hollowed in the back. The house pillars were made concave so that they could be cupped against the true supports which were not decorated. This feature of the Tlingit house pillar was a distinct advantage over that of the Haida, in that the elaborately-carved and expensive posts could be retrieved when the

house got beyond repair. In that case the old posts were again set up in the new building. A fine set of four house posts brought to Wrangell from Kotslitan after 1834 and placed in a new community house there may still be seen in the reconstructed Chief Shakes community house on Shakes Island in the inner harbor. Similarly, in Klukwan are some beautiful old house pillars that formerly stood in earlier houses now lost through decay or destroyed by the meandering Chilkat river.

In most instances painting waited until the entire pole was carved. However, the writer recalls a Kwakiutl carver at Alert Bay who had completed only the uppermost figure of his pole and was in the act of painting it before proceeding with the rest of the carving. It was quite likely that he was being paid upon the completion of each figure rather than having to wait for his pay until the entire pole was finished.

As recorded in an earlier chapter, totem poles were painted originally with paints of native manufacture. Those made from mineral pigments derived from carbon, iron and copper oxides were beautiful and enduring. Others made from various colored earths soon faded out. As mentioned elsewhere, these pigments were mixed with masticated salmon eggs to produce an enduring tempera in soft pastel shades. Perhaps none of these paints have come down to us in their original form since they must have been adulterated as early as the last quarter of the 18th century. Traces of mercuric sulphide have been found in ancient burials which may have been British or Chinese vermilion brought in by the earliest traders. The lively red seen by Meares and Vancouver must have been vermilion or a combination of vermilion and red oxide, the imported ver-

CARVING A POLE. Native artisans of the Rehabilitation Project at work on a large pole at Saxman. "Photo by Schallerer."

RAISING A POLE. The late Chief Shakes VII, better known as plain "Charley Jones" supervises the raising of a tall totem pole on his ancestral island. Kake natives, his honored guests, are assisting. Wrangell Potlatch 1940.

Photo by author.

milion being used to brighten the duller local oxides. In fairly recent times the use of boat paints on both totem poles and heraldic screens made those so painted gaudy and barbarous, requiring some years of weathering to restore the quiet beauty of the original monuments.

If it has been sufficiently demonstrated in the preceding chapters that tall, ornate totem poles are not ancient, in fact, a development occasioned since and undoubtedly by the introduction of steel, then it would be paradoxical to attempt to account for the carving and erection of totem poles by some original primitive means. Writers have made much of the fact that these monuments were erected in a manner similar to that employed by the Polynesians, implying that these Northwest Coast islands were peopled originally by Hawaiians in a migration such as that of the Samoans to New Zealand, whence sprang the Maori. However, no such theory is warranted or even necessary, for the several cultural similarities between the Haida and Hawaiian are easily accounted for by recent acculturation. The record clearly shows that the phenomenal development of sculpture and architecture among the Haida and Tsimshian closely parallels the activity of Northwest Coast traders and their part Polynesian crews.

The Reverend Jonathan S. Green, missionary from Hawaii who visited the Northwest Coast in 1829 on a trading ship for the purpose of examining the area as a potential missionary field, gives an excellent picture of the district lying between Sitka and the Queen Charlotte Islands and the people residing there. Travelling on the bark "Volunteer," Captain Charles Taylor, out of *Honoruru*, Sandwich Islands, he spent an entire season between Sitka, Kaigani, Tongass, Nass River, Massett, and Skidegate, calling in at each place repeatedly as the skipper traded for furs.

As early as that, Green wrote, "For more than forty years, our enterprising countrymen have coasted these shores, and realized immense profits from their commercial intercourse with the natives. . . ." In other words, long before the Russians established old Sitka (1799), Americans out of Boston and Salem, and British, French and Spanish as well, were trading in the Alaska Panhandle and Coastal British Columbia, and perhaps in every instance coming in via Hawaii. Their deck crews were made up largely of Northwest Coast Indians and Polynesians who intermingled freely, aboard and ashore, and Polynesians married Indian girls and settled down. Even today one can see their shadows in all coastal Indian tribes but especially in the Haida where some of the girls could pass for Maori and wavy-haired men resemble full-muscled Samoans and Hawaiians. Barbeau mentions a part-Hawaiian totem carver named *Oyai* who was regarded as the best carver on the Nass. Just which part of his ancestry contributed the most to his skill is a moot question for it is likely that the Polynesians learned as much from the Indians as the Indians did from them. Rev. Jonathan Green, for one, regarded the culture of the Northwest Coast Indians on a higher plane than in any of the south sea islands, including Hawaii and New Zealand, suggesting that if there were any borrowing, it was the Maori who took home ideas they had acquired in association with the Haida.

In trying to visualize these Northwest Coast natives, one should avoid the error of thinking of them as American Indians of other parts who are likely to be stolid and taciturn, emotionless, and slow to adopt new ideas. Quite the opposite, these

THE OLD AND THE NEW. Demonstrating the amount of rigging required in erecting a sixty-five foot totem pole. Wrangell, 1940. Photo by author.

coastal Indians, particularly the Haida and Coast Tsimshian, were mentally alert, physically active and exceedingly garrulous. A little insight into the character of these people of that day may be gained from Green's diary of June 25, 1829. He wrote, "The sun shines from about three a.m. until nearly nine p.m. and yet the days are not sufficiently long for the Indians to do their talking. My patience is exceedingly tried. The *Skidegas* men exceed all that I have yet seen for keenness in trade. One reason is that their skins are the sea-otter, there being very little land fur on the island. One of these skins is worth more than ten beavers, and being scarce and eagerly sought, the man who has taken one calculates to banter at least two days before he sells it, and during this time he claims special privileges, expects that he shall have free access to the cabin to eat, drink, and lounge, and he must have things in style, too, or he will be highly offended. They make a regular business of bantering—talk till they are weary—take a short nap on deck or in the cabin—after which they will resume the business with renewed vigor. So uniformly do those Indians torment us when they have these skins, that I dread to see one brought over the side of the ship."

The Reverend Mr. Green observed *busts* and *carved masts* at Kaigani during his several visits there in 1829. He perhaps did not know that his countryman, Captain Roberts of the *Jefferson* helped raise a totem pole in this same village thirty-five years earlier. Competition between the traders being what it was, the Indians made the most of it. On this occasion in 1794 the Captain and his crewmen planed, sanded, painted and erected the totem pole at the request of a local chief, the pole being raised with the aid of two spare topmasts and the necessary tackle.

This is not the only instance reported, wherein white man and Polynesian assisted in raising totem poles more than a hundred years ago. Barbeau records such assistance given the Nass river natives and calls attention to the fact that the *trench* method of raising a tall totem pole is identical with that of south sea islanders.

The trench method consists of digging a trench some twenty feet in length, starting shallow and gradually sloping it to the other end which will be of the depth at which it is intended to set the pole. The pole is rolled into the trench with the butt in the deep end where it lies at about a thirty degree angle. A short log roller is placed under the upper end and is moved forward as the pole is raised by straight lifting, and the use of *scissors* and pikes. A plank standing upright at the far side of the hole prevents gouging and aids in getting the pole erect. Then the whole band, men, women, and children complete the job with lines, while a foreman sitting on a nearby stump or housetop shouts out the native equivalent of "Yo, heave!" Once erect, the totem pole is twisted about until it faces the proper direction, that is, the waterfront, then the trench and hole are filled in.

Block and tackle hoisting equipment is used when available, which probably means ever since the advent of white man's sailing ships. Tall poles are set much shallower than one would expect, due to the presence of shallow bedrock, and this no doubt accounts for the many poles seen leaning before their time.

111

MUNGO MARTIN AT WORK. This close-up gives a good idea of the relative size of totem poles as well as a glimpse of the intricate texturing accomplished by the adze. Here the carver is using the crooked knife for fine carving.   Provincial Museum, Victoria, B.C. photo

Chapter Twelve

TOTEM POLE RESTORATION

Had the monuments erected on the Northwest Coast in the past hundred years been carved of stone instead of cedar, the problem of restoration might well have rested until sometime in the next millennium. In fact, had even the circumstances attendant to the raising of these sculptured pillars been different, there is no question but that they could have been preserved a hundred or more years beyond their natural lifetime. Or had the culture that called them into being continued, new and finer totem poles would have rendered unnecessary the preservation of those that preceded.

Such, however, was not to be the case. As has been brought out earlier, a totem pole was carved and erected with great ceremony and at tremendous expense. Once he had acquitted himself of all obligations attendant to the raising of a memorial, the chief was not required or even expected ever to repair the pole. If he did desire to repaint, move, straighten, or otherwise alter a memorial once erected he could not do so except through the medium of a ceremony and at the same expense as if he were erecting a new pole. All the work would have to be done by the members of the opposite phratry who would have to be paid for their labor. Guests would be invited to attend the alteration ceremony out of courtesy and would receive presents from the host. For all of this effort and expense, the host could expect to receive no new honors. It is manifestly clear that even in earlier times there was little, if any, incentive for the preservation of totem poles where the owner gained no new honor and no prestige. Even to restore the totem pole of a predecessor would likewise in no way enhance the reputation of the individual interested in preserving the monument.

The net result was that through the conspiracy of climate and social usage a cedar totem pole could hardly be expected to stand much longer than the man it honored. So long as new poles replaced those rotting away there seemed no need to be concerned lest this unique art disappear from the earth. Yet when totem-carving practically ceased at the turn of the century, it was plain that unless something was done soon to preserve those monuments left standing, it would be but a question of a few years when there would not be a single totem pole left standing *in situ* on the whole Northwest Coast.

While a great many totem poles had been removed from their original settings to grace the parks and museums of the United States, Canada, Alaska and even Europe, the first recorded instance of an effort to preserve totem clusters in Alaska, intact, was in Sitka. A *Public Park* was

113

RECLAMATION: the forest advances to reclaim its own and soon all vestiges of man's handiwork is lost.   U.S.F.S. Phot

created there by proclamation on June 21, 1890 on the site of the old *Kiksadi* Indian village and fort, where in 1804 the battle for Sitka was won by the Russians, and where a cluster of totem poles had been set up by Governor Brady a hundred years later. This park became the Sitka National Monument on March 23, 1910 by the Executive Order of President William Howard Taft because "under general laws of Alaska it had been found difficult to prevent vandalism within the area."

The National Monument of Old Kasaan (since abandoned) was originally established by Executive Order in 1907 amplified by the Presidential Proclamation of Oct. 25, 1916. It contained an area of some 40 acres embracing the Haida village of Kasaan on Skowl Arm of Kasaan Bay. It is about 40 miles east of Ketchikan on Prince of Wales Island. The village, deserted since 1900, contained many fine totem poles and the ruins of community houses.

In the spring of 1926, Dr. H. W. Krieger of the U.S. National Museum on loan to the Bureau of American Ethnology, was detailed to inspect the houses and totem poles at Old Kasaan with a view to their preservation. He found many of the poles beyond repair but the remaining monuments were scraped and treated with creosote. He did not consider the expense of repainting the poles justified "unless tourist travel should increase materially and a caretaker could be maintained to keep down the alders and salmon berry brush so as to prevent any future danger of destruction by fire during the short dry season in the fall of the year."

The late Honorable Judge James Wickersham as early as 1920 had started a movement aimed at the preservation of the totem monuments at Port Tongass where the Abraham Lincoln totem pole stood. In 1923 on the occasion of President Harding's visit to Alaska he sought to have the President's itinerary altered to include a visit to that historic spot. He held the conviction that if President Harding could but see the Great Emancipator's totem pole he would order the island made a National Monument. The itinerary, however, was not changed and the Lincoln totem pole, together with the rest, continued to decay unseen for sixteen years longer.

About the same time (1920) General James Gordon Steese, then President of the Alaska Road Commission, upon finding several of the Sitka totem poles down, initiated a movement to have the poles raised and repainted. At his request, and through the office of Alaska's Governor Thomas Riggs, $200 was appropriated in 1921 for this work by the National Park Service, the job being supervised by the Alaska Road Commission.

In the years intervening between 1921 and 1938

CHIEF SHAKES' COMMUNITY HOUSE. This restoration on a tiny islet in Wrangell's inner harbor is within ten minutes walk from the steamer docks. It is by far the most popular attraction in the Totem Town.

(U.S. Forest Service Photo)

THE *TIRED WOLF* HOUSE POST. Shown here is an example of the tremendous effort made by the U.S. Forest Service to save badly-rotted pillars and poles by insetting pieces with pegs wherever the wood was too deeply rotted to save.

restoration of Alaska's totem poles was a sporadic enterprise carried out by a few far-seeing individuals or by local service clubs such as the Wrangell Chamber of Commerce and the Ketchikan American Legion Post. The late Walter Waters of Wrangell purchased several poles and totem figures and moved them from deserted West Coast villages to Wrangell where they stood for many years. Some he preserved from dry rot by the liberal use of rock salt introduced through holes bored in the top.

Others, already badly rotted in spots, he repaired by removing the rotted wood, refilling the cavities with concrete, and re-painting. In other instances sections of new wood were set in and held by means of dowels.

Since the Totempolar Region of Alaska is entirely within the confines of the Tongass National Forest, it early became apparent that any concerted effort to restore the totem poles left standing in deserted Indian villages would have to be under the jurisdiction of the U.S. Forest Service which was excellently staffed for this sort of undertaking and had the necessary boats, shops, tools and equipment to do the job.

In 1921 Regional Forester Charles Flory in a letter to his Chief lamented the deterioration of the totem poles and recommended moving them to a central location for rehabilitation. Four years later he addressed a similar letter to Governor George Parks. No action was taken in either instance and the matter rested there until in 1934 when Flory reviewed the past correspondence and recommended that natives be used under some relief act to move and rehabilitate the totem poles. Lengthy discussions of the matter followed but no project crystallized out of the mass of paper work.

In February 1937, Dr. Ernest Gruening, then Director of Territories and Insular Possessions, reopened the question by recommending to Chief Forester Silcox that something be done to preserve the poles. During the greater part of the next two years the Forest Service collected data on location and condition of existing totem poles and community houses, the rightful owners of them and ways and means of securing title so that they could be moved to various centers for rehabilitation if and when such a project be instituted.

The program of totem pole restoration was actually initiated as a Civilian Conservation Corps, Indian Division, project in July 1938 by Regional Forester B. Frank Heintzleman who was also Director for the Alaska C.C.C. In addition to $127,492 of C.C.C. funds, $42,878 was expended from funds of the Emergency Relief Administration under the direction of the C.C.C. officials.

In this project which did not formally close until June 30, 1942, approximately 250 Indians were employed. Totem poles from Cape Fox, Old Tongass Village, Village Island, Pennock Island, Old Kasaan, Sukkwan, Klinkwan, Howkan, Tuxekan, Seattle, Sitka, Wrangell and Ketchikan were removed for restoration or duplication. It is interesting to note here, that Seattle's famous Pioneer's Square totem pole, purloined from Old Tongass Village in 1899, was duplicated for Seattle by the descendants of the Indians from it was stolen on that memorable *Good Will* excursion.

Since many of the above sites were in hidden *canoe harbors* seldom visited by anyone, most of the renovated poles were set up in clusters in the more accessible places, especially in the towns where the descendants of the old totem carvers now reside. Hence, clusters were erected at New Kasaan, Saxman and Totem Bight near Ketchikan, Hydaburg, Klawock, Wrangell and Sitka, forming unique totem pole parks in those communities.

Individual totem poles were set up in Ketchikan, Wrangell, Juneau, Old Auke Village Site near Juneau, Sitka and Seattle. In all, 48 old poles were restored, another 54 beyond restoration were duplicated by native artisans and 19 poles which existed only in memory were carved anew. Besides, three Indian community houses were duplicated: one at Totem Bight, another at Kasaan, and a third on Shakes Island in Wrangell's inner harbor.

Although the project was initiated, directed and carried out by the U.S. Forest Service, it had the co-operation of the U.S. Indian Service, the Alaska Governor's Office, many other interested public agencies and individuals, both white and native. Through it a cross-section of the most remarkable native art in America has been preserved for public enjoyment for many years to come.

One fact demonstrated by the Forest Service project and in native art projects at Wrangell Institute, Sheldon Jackson School and the Ketchikan Indian School was that the art of totem pole carving was not dead. Natives of the Northwest Coast have an innate artistic sense and many are naturalborn wood workers. Given a new incentive and a fair recompense there is no question but that a great contribution to the plastic art of America could again come from the Northwest Coast.

In the Canadian section of the Totempolar Region, restoration projects have been carried on to a certain extent for many years. Up until 1925 the policy was to acquire totem poles from deserted villages in out-of-the-way places and bring them to Victoria or Vancouver where they would be restored, then placed in storage, in museums or in public parks. British Columbia was fortunate in having within the confines of its borders the principal seats of all the totem pole carving tribes except the Tlingit. Thus it has been able to restore a much more representative display than could be had in Alaska where only the Tlingit and the Kaigani branch of the Haida carved these cedar monuments.

Prominent in the work of totem pole preservation and restoration in British Columbia is the Art-

CHIEF EDENSHAW'S TOTEM POLE. Brought from Massett, Queen Charlotte Islands, this pole now graces Prince Rupert's Totem Pole Park. It is perhaps the widest pole ever carved by the Haidas. Figures which once capped the pole have rotted away as has the lower portion through which the house was entered.

(Photo by author).

117

DUK-TOOTHL OR KA-HA-SI TOTEM POLE. This Memorial stood at the rear of Shakes' Community House on Shakes Island in Wrangell's Inner Harbor. It tells the classic story of the weakling who became the Strong Man. (See Story)
(Photo by the author).

Historical and Scientific Association of Vancouver. Founded originally in 1889 it took its present form in 1894. Besides operating the Vancouver Public Museum, the Association is responsible for placing the totem poles in Stanley Park. Of these, the first were obtained in 1926 and set up by the Parks Board at *Lumberman's Arch.* The *Chief Wakius* totem pole from Alert Bay was purchased for $700.00, the funds being raised by popular subscription. The *Sisa-kaulas* pole from Kingcombe Inlet was presented to the city by Mr. W. C. Shelly, a Parks Board member. Two house posts were also set up at that time.

On the occasion of Vancouver's Golden Jubilee the Thunderbird pole was set up at Prospect Point and the *Dsoo-kwa-dsi, Nhe-is-bik,* and *Ske-dans* poles added to the cluster at Lumberman's Arch. These poles were presented to the City of Vancouver on August 25, 1936, jointly by the Jubilee Committee and the Indian Department.

All of these poles are of Kwakiutl origin except the Ske-dans mortuary pole which is Haida, having been erected originally at Skidegate, Queen Charlotte Islands about eighty years ago.

The most ambitious totem pole restoration project conducted in British Columbia was for the preservation of the poles along the Skeena River. Begun in 1925 and carried on through 1926, the project was the joint enterprise of Canadian Indian Affairs, Mines, National Parks, and the National Museum with the co-operation of the Canadian National Railways. The Department of Indian Affairs defrayed all the running expenses and the National Railways supplied quantities of material free of charge plus the services of a special engineer.

Owing to the fact that Canada had outlawed the Potlatch, thus indirectly prohibiting the erection of totem poles, the party had considerable initial difficulty with the Indians in securing permission to restore the poles. "Why," they asked, "do you wish to preserve totem poles which only a few years ago you forbade us to erect?"

Good will and consent were eventually gained and the work commenced. Poles, decayed at their bases, were cut off at ground level and bolted to new bases which were treated with creosote. Then the old portions were repainted. Finally the poles were set in concrete, capped with plastic gum to prevent seepage between wood and concrete. Although the freshly-painted poles appeared gaudy at first, they soon faded, restoring the original and much-desired archaic appearance.

In his report on this project, published in 1926, Harlan I. Smith, Dominion Archaeologist, stated, "Ninety per cent of the totem-poles at Kitwanga are now restored. Only two remain untouched, and for these the native owner refuses to give his consent. The Indians have given permission to work on eight poles at Gitseyukla, one at Hazelton, four at Hagwelget, and two at the forbidden village of Kitwinkul; it is understood, also, that they agree to the restoration of all the poles at Kispiox."

Nowhere on the coast has such effective use been made of cedar monuments as in Prince Rupert where handsome Haida poles have been set with great artistry amid the rocky hillocks which account for much of that city's wild beauty. Here again through the co-operation of several agencies priceless mementos of a dead artistic past have been preserved for our enjoyment for many years to come. In this instance the City Council, the Indian Office and the Canadian National Railways worked together. Mr. J. Gillett, Indian Agent, selected the poles from the villages of Skidegate and Massett, established ownership of them and secured the donor's names so that they might appear on the poles when erected. Steamships of the Canadian National Railways brought the poles to Prince Rupert in 1935 free of charge. The City Council financed rehabilitation and erection, the painting being done by the late William Beynon, well-known as an authority on local Indian customs. Thirteen poles in all were erected, among them the Edenshaw pole from Massett, possibly the widest pole ever erected, and another which would rank among the very tallest. Later several more were brought in from the islands, two of which stand before the Navy Building.

Another restoration project of British Columbia totem poles was accomplished in 1940-41 resulting in the establishment of Thunderbird Park in the capitol city of Victoria. This project was an activity of the Provincial Museum working on a special grant with the co-operation of the City Council which provided the park area.

Most of the poles erected in this new park had long been lying in storage in the Old Drill Hall on Menzies Street, others having been purchased recently. Here were erected totem poles, grave figures, and house fronts of the Haida, Kwakiutl, Nootka and Salish peoples. Effectively placed against a natural forest background and floodlighted at night, the new park soon became a tourist mecca.

In 1952 a three-year totem pole restoration project was undertaken under the direction of Wilson Duff, Provincial Anthropologist for the purpose of replacing decaying poles displayed out-of-doors so that the fine originals could be taken down and preserved indefinitely indoors. Three exhibits were completed that year by Mungo Martin, veteran Kwakiutl carver assisted by his son, David. A fourth

REAR VIEW OF DUK-TOOTHL MORTUARY POLE. Showing cavities for receiving ashes of the dead. Only the high caste Tlingits received this type of burial.

(Photo by the author).

THE NEW DUK-TOOTHL (Black Skin) or KA-HA-SI MORTUARY POLE. When the old pole got beyond repair, a new one was carved by Indians under the direction of the U.S. Forest Service.

(Photo by the author).

was in progress. The following year saw the construction of a full-sized Kwakiutl community house which was erected in Thunderbird Park, the carving on the front of which represents a supernatural sea-monster in the form of a sculpin.

In 1954 Mungo Martin, David Martin and Henry Hunt produced replicas of two Haida, two Tsimshian, one Kwakiutl and one Bella Coola totem poles. The next year thirteen poles were erected in Thunderbird Park and four Haida and one Kwakiutl pole were carved. The Victoria Daily Times organized a community project to employ the carvers for three months to carve the world's tallest totem pole to be given to the City of Victoria when completed. This year saw the park filled and the newly carved surplus poles were stored to await assignment to suitable locations elsewhere in the Province.

The year 1956 saw the world's tallest totem pole which bears 127 feet 7 inches of carving, erected in Beacon Hill Park, Victoria, and formally dedicated on July 2nd of that year. The Beaver pole was placed in Exposition Park, Vancouver, and the Skedans Grisly Bear pole was set up at Peace Arch Park.

The year 1957 saw the carving of a 100 foot pole to be sent to London as a Centennial gift as well as a replica of it for the City of Vancouver. The following year the Centennial pole was erected in Great Windsor Park in London and its replica in Haddon Park, Vancouver. The year also saw a start on the copying of three Tsimshian poles from Kitwancool acquired on a "new pole for an old pole" basis.

Begun in 1959 and completed early the next year was a 60 foot pole commissioned by the Boy Scouts National Association for the new headquarters in Ottawa, the pole being an integral architectural feature of the building. During 1960 Henry Holt carved a new Thunderbird with ten foot wing-spread for the Thunderbird Park arch. In 1961 a pair of 15 foot poles were carved to be incorporated in the entrance portal of Rebecca Spit Park.

Recently a 37 foot pole commissioned by the Canadian Government was erected in Mexico as a gift to the people of Mexico and as we go to press a 65 foot pole is being carved for the Canadian Embassy in Argentina, to stand in Plaza Canada, Buenos Aires.

In addition to the restoration of a ten year period above enumerated a pole was restored and re-erected on a steel and concrete base beside the museum at Hazelton (1960) and as a Centennial project the totem poles at Alert bay were restored (1958).

The University of British Columbia at Vancouver has been the scene of the most significant work in restoration and carving in recent years. Between the years 1947 and 1951, Mungo Martin set up a Kwakiutl section which established the Totem Park on the campus. Over the years between 1954 and the present (1963), half of the old totem poles salvaged from the old coastal villages have gone to the University. About 1960 they built a storage-workshop, and over the next two years, with the help of Canada Council grants, they had a major carving program and set up a Haida section. The carvers were Bill Reid, of Haida descent, and Doug Cranmer, a Kwakiutl. The Haida unit consists of a massive house and a small mortuary house, one

inside house post, two frontal poles, two different kinds of mortuary poles, a memorial pole, and a memorial figure. The poles are not straight copies of old poles, but were designed by Reid. However, they are purely Haida and "quite the most magnificent Haida poles ever carved" according to Wilson Duff.

Compared to the amazing accomplishments in totem pole restoration achieved in British Columbia in the past decade or so, Alaskan efforts seem quite insignificant. In most instances it has been difficult even to marshal enough enthusiasm to maintain the gains made under the C.C.C. twenty years ago. Lately, however, under Statehood and because of a rapidly developing tourist resource, more interest is being taken in these picturesque relics of a past culture.

In the Sitka National Monument, the thirteen totem poles to be seen there are kept in first class condition by the local management who also pro-

THE NEW LINCOLN TOTEM POLE. A poor copy of the original pole that stood on Tongass Island, this memorial to Abraham Lincoln may be seen in Totem Park, Saxman, about two miles from Ketchikan. Because the Lincoln figure on this replica is carved in a stylized manner rather than realistically as in the original, many people have come to doubt that Lincoln actually was intended. However a Brady photo of Lincoln at Antietam, showing Lincoln standing in high hat and with arms akimbo as in the totem pole, is believed to have been the carver's model.

U.S. Forest Service Photo.

FIGURE OF ABRAHAM LINCOLN. It once surmounted the Lincoln totem pole. The two men are Tlingit carvers who helped carve the new pole. The figure may be seen in the State Museum in Juneau.

U.S. Forest Service Photo.

vide a brochure which gives a brief account of each pole. Lately the Kiksadi Indian fort, *Shish-kee-nu,* or "Sapling Fort," has been re-located by archaeological survey and its outlines delineated. It was there that in 1804 the Kiksadis were defeated by the Russians, making it possible for Alexander Baranof to establish his capital on this site and build Novo Archanglsk, known today as Sitka.

At the several villages, namely Hydaburg, Klawock, Saxman and Kasaan, where totem pole clusters had been set up more than twenty years ago, some maintenance has been provided lately through work parties financed by the Division of Rural Affairs of the State of Alaska. This work has consisted mainly of brushing out, weed cutting, making and maintaining paths and bridges and in extending roads. A plan was under way to have all of the poles in these parks restored and repainted in 1963.

A replica of an Indian community house, 40 feet by 44 feet, was completed and dedicated in August 1962 at Port Chilkoot. This was a project of Alaska Indian Arts, Inc. a teen-age group organized in 1957 under the leadership of Carl Heinmiller for the purpose of reviving local Indian Dances. Known as the Chilkat Dancers, this group has inspired other dancers, notably of Yakutat, to revive their tribal dances and to put on exhibitions at various gatherings throughout the state. As a by-product of the revival of native dances is the production of headdresses, wooden masks, and rattles and other paraphrenalia used in these theatricals.

Juneau, which had never boasted of more than three totem poles in the past, gained another in 1963 through the efforts of the local Rotary Club. This is a Haida story pole about 45 feet tall, surplus from the Hydaburg cluster. It displays four stories from Haida mythology. Set up in a small park at the head of Seward street, this pole may be seen for several blocks.

Another significant gain for Northwest Coast art was the State of Alaska's decision to specify the

RUINS OF A HAIDA HOUSE AT OLD KASAAN. These fine interior house pillars have been restored and incorporated into a Haida Community House Restoration at Kasaan by the U.S. Forest Service.

U.S. Forest Service Photo.

HYDABURG TOTEM PARK. Contains restored totem poles from abandoned Haida villages of Klinkwan, Howkan and Sukkwan.

U.S. Forest Service Photo

KLAWOCK TOTEM PARK. Contains restored poles from Tuxikan, old Tlingit village on West Coast of Prince of Wales Island.

U.S. Forest Service Photo

decor of its new ferries which operate on the marine highway between Prince Rupert and Skagway, to be in the traditional local Indian style. This was accomplished with excellent results.

Even though most of the fine old totem poles are gone, there are enough good photographs of them available to make it possible to reproduce them accurately and a program for carving these duplicates similar to that in British Columbia should be gotten under way without delay. The Alaska Centennial in 1967 should be the inspiration for restoration programs of this nature through the entire Totempolar Region.

A LONE TOTEMIC BEAR, BUT NOT ENTIRELY ALONE. Other totems may be seen blending with the forest in the background.

U.S.F.S. Photo.

SALVAGING TOTEM POLES ON ANTHONY ISLAND, B.C. One can better appreciate the heroic efforts that go into totem pole salvage at an abandoned site on a remote island from such a view. Many poles still standing in Alaska and British Columbia are too rotted to be moved. This work is under direction of the University of British Columbia.

British Columbia Government Photograph

TWO MASSIVE RAVENS MARK A SAXMAN TOTEM PARK ENTRANCE. In the background are the Owl and Raven poles. A woman who was cruel to her blind mother-in-law was punished by being changed into an owl. Her descendants took Owl as their crest. The animal at the base of the pole is Weasel.

A CLOSE-UP OF RAVEN: trickster diety, benefactor of man, phratry symbol, leading character of a hundred tales.
U.S.F.S. Photo.

THE CHIEF EBBETS MEMORIAL POLE. Featuring the Bear and Shark clan symbols. This pole erected after 1880 honors the chief who erected the Lincoln Totem Pole some ten or twelve years earlier.

U.S.F.S. Photo.

FLYING RAVEN POLE IN THE SAXMAN TOTEM PARK. This is a Tlingit pole, unusual with its outspread wings which is generally the exclusive feature of the Kwakiutl.

U.S.F.S. Photo.

TWO HAIDA POLES. Carved under the direction of Haida master carver, John Wallace, and erected at Totem Bight near Ketchikan. The first tells the story of the Master Artisan and the second, another version of the Wasgo legend. Original stood at Klinkwan.

U.S.F.S. Photo.

Haida pole carved under the direction of John Wallace, Master Haida carver. Erected at Totem Bight, near Ketchikan, it tells the story of the "Master Artisan."
U.S.F.S. Photo.

ENTRANCE TO THE SAXMAN TOTEM PARK. This time guarded by bears.
U.S.F.S. Photo.

Chapter Thirteen

THE HERALDIC SCREEN

While the Northwest Coast totem poles are undoubtedly known the world over, they had relatives just beyond the range of the tall red cedars that are known to only a few specialists and the local residents. These are the *heraldic screens* which, altho not entirely unknown to Tsimshian, Haida, Kwakiutl and Nootka, are largely confined to the villages of the northern Tlingit.

Heraldic screens may be defined as any of those carved and painted, or simply painted, wall panels or partitions found at the rear of named community houses and bearing decorations illustrating tribal legends relative to the occupants of the house. In other words, these screens took the place of the heraldic poles of tribes farther south which commonly told similar stories on cedar poles rather than rectangular screens made of boards.

The two best known of these heraldic screens are the *Bear Screen* from the Chief Shakes Community House at Wrangell, now the property of the Denver Art Museum and on display in Chappell House, and the *Rainwall Screen* in the Whale House in Klukwan, Alaska. Wolfgang Paalen, who once owned the Bear Screen, considered it "perhaps the finest and oldest of the five or six existing pieces of this kind." George T. Emmons, in complimenting Paalen on his purchase said, "you are fortunate in getting this piece, as such carved and painted screens were only to be found in half a dozen of the chief's houses in Southeastern Alaska . . ."

Emmons, in 1916, describing the Chilkat Whale House which was built about or before 1835, made this statement about the Rainwall screen behind which was the chief's apartment, "It is unquestionably the finest example of native art, either Tlingit or Tsimshian, in Alaska, in boldness of conception,—although highly conventionalized—in execution of detail, and in the selection and arrangement of colors."

Since this early screen probably has within it the secret of the origin of all subsequent heraldic screens found on the Northwest Coast, it has been selected for the honor of *prototype* especially since its forebears are clear both in legend and in demonstrable fact.

In his monograph on the Chilkat Blanket Emmons says, "The apron or waist robe is a blanket in miniature, a reproduction in weaving of the shaman's skin waist robe from which it derives its name. It was unquestionably the earliest product of the loom in this material and type of weaving and in the course of years it grew to the size of a blanket. . . . The Chilkat story of its origin says that long ago there lived on the Skeena River in British Columbia, a Tsimshian

131

woman, a widow, of the village of Kitkatla, and her only daughter, *Hi-you-was-clar* (rain mother). It had been a season of extreme want. The deep snows of winter still covered the lowlands, and the spirit of hunger stalked abroad as a famished wolf. Day after day the girl sat, half dazed from want of food, staring vacantly at the intricately-carved and painted picture that covered the rear interior partition of the house; for, although poor, they were of high caste, and their surroundings spoke of past greatness. The picture finally took possession of her and, setting up a rude frame, she forgot her suffering, and lost herself in the work of weaving

an apron of like design. Later her hand was sought by the son of the chief and, in the exchange of presents her handiwork was given to the father-in-law who honored the occasion by giving a great feast at which he wore the apron, and sacrificed many slaves in token of his appreciation of the gift. Its fame spread abroad and strangers came from afar to see it; and in time it was copied, until the Tsimshian became the acknowledged weavers of the coast."

This Chilkat story seems to establish two things, at least in the minds of the Chilkat. First, that the prototype of the Chilkat blanket was a shaman's

INTERIOR VIEW OF THE WHALE HOUSE AT KLUKWAN (1895). This view shows the famous *Rain Wall* heraldic screen behind which were the chief's quarters. The screen depicts the *Gonakadate* rising from the sea with water pouring from his outstretched arms. Encircling the central figure are personified raindrops, dancing as they strike and rebound.

The man standing at the far left has his left hand resting on the *Woodworm* bowl, a potlatch dish 14 feet long. The three boys at the rear are wearing as hats, the woven cedar bark cases made to protect and shield from profane eyes, the jointed tribal spruce root hats worn by the man at the left and the two in the foreground.

The house pillar at the left is called the *Woodworm Post* and recalls the story of the girl who suckled a woodworm. Two woodworms form her headdress, while a third is held against her breast. Beneath the girl is *Mosquito* in the act of biting *Frog*, and recalling the Cannibal Giant story. (See story)

The pillar to the right of the screen is *Raven Post*, and recalls the *Barbecue Raven* story. The upper figure is *Raven* in human form, holding in his two hands a personified jade adze. The bottom figure which looks like the head of a sculpin or bull head is actually supposed to represent the king salmon which Raven barbecued. The bird occupying the space between the two large heads is issuing from *Raven's* mouth and symbolizes *Raven Telling Lies* as he did to the small birds who helped with the barbecue and were cheated out of their share. (See Barbecue Raven story.)

Photo by Lloyd Winter.

apron and second, that the originators of the Chilkat Blanket were Tsimshian. Another story, also from Emmons, tells how the art of blanket weaving came to the Chilkat and hints of the origin of the Rainwall. Speaking of the peregrinations of the Chilkats, Emmons says: "Southward they made annual trips to the country of the Tsimshian to purchase slaves, war canoes, and red-cedar chests. On one of those excursions a blanket was obtained which the two wives of the old chief unraveled and studied until they learned the weave. But they could not utilize their knowledge as they had no pattern board to guide them. One night the elder wife dreamed of a beautiful blanket with many tiny white figures resembling raindrops scattered over it. She said the spirits wished her to weave a blanket like it, but that she could not do it without a pattern board. Now, the Tsimshian were recognized as the best weavers of the coast as well as the most artistic people and the chief said that she should go to them and tell her dream to a designer who would reproduce it on a pattern board. This was done and when they returned home the two wives wove a ceremonial robe for their lord which was the first produced by the people."

Whether such a blanket was ever made or not is beside the point but the relationship between the Rainwall of the Whale House and this mythological pattern board is at once apparent. Whoever designed this screen had taken a typical Tsimshian cedar treasure chest front panel decoration, liberally sprinkled it with personified raindrops and bordered it with more frog-like raindrops. Emmons calls the central figure the *Rain Spirit* but this interpretation is seriously questioned by Tlingits generally. At least one reliable Tlingit informant avers it depicts the *Gonakadet* in the act of rising from the sea, the wing-like appendages to its arms representing water falling away. Another denies that it represents a rain spirit as such a spirit is unrecognized by the Tlingit and others bear the same conviction. Emmons in his Chilkat Blanket paper describes the *Gonakadet* in its various fancied forms, one of which so aptly describes the Rainwall design that it is a wonder he did not recognize it himself when he wrote his Whale House paper some eight or ten years later. He says, "The belief in the mythical being, *Gonakadet*, occurs along the whole coast. He lives in the sea, and brings power and fortune to all who see him. Sometimes he rises out of the water as a beautifully painted house front inlaid with the much-prized blue and green haliotis shell, again as the head of an immense fish or as an elaborately painted war canoe. In decorative art he is generally represented as a large head

THE KADJUK SCREEN FROM THE YAKUTAT DRUM HOUSE. This is a good example of the type of art that flourished briefly after gold was discovered near Juneau in 1880. Made in Sitka after 1900 of sawn boards in random widths, it is framed with commercial moulding and studded with brass tacks inspired by the Chinese camphorwood chests that had lately displaced the native cedar chests. The bottom composition of eyes and a face represent a personified mountain on which it appears two marmots crouch. Actually there is only one, repeated for balance. The mythological *Kadjuk* stands, with broken wing, singing a death song on the mountain top. The animals at left and right are heralding the coming of the dawn. The small faces above are clouds but actually are there only to represent the *North Wind* which, being invisible, is recognized only by the form of the clouds in art.

The artist got into serious trouble with Kadjuk's legs and feet, depicting them realistically and botching an otherwise excellent composition. (See Story)

with arms, paws, and fins." The accompanying photograph of the Rainwall shows a chief's chest of similar design, being inlaid with opercula and haliotis shell as was the heraldic screen which was the Tsimshian maiden's inspiration for the original Chilkat blanket, or at least of its pattern board.

Bentwood boxes were in general use along the entire Northwest Coast at the time of discovery of these peoples by Europeans, since they took the place of pottery vessels used by most Indians, and all other receptacles except baskets. If it seems reasonable that Chilkat blankets were inspired by heraldic screens, it would be even more reasonable to assume that the screens, in turn, were derived from earlier bentwood boxes or chief's treasure chests since they were traded from tribe to tribe regardless of linguistic group, and thus had a much greater distribution.

THUNDERBIRD HERALDIC SCREEN FROM YAKUTAT. This screen, made on order in Juneau in 1905, of tongue and groove ceiling material, boasts a carved center piece. The assembly of faces represents clouds, depict a storm out of which comes Thunderbird, the personified thunder and lightning. The human figure repeated below represents a small boy who, having strayed from his family on a canoe trip down the Alsek River, was lost then rescued by Thunderbird. Believing that he had been abandoned by his people, Thunderbird was at the point of changing the boy into a Thunderbird like himself when he was found by his parents standing between the legs of his captor. Already pinfeathers were appearing along his arms and legs. After much discussion he was finally ransomed on the condition that a house be built in Yakutat in honor of Thunderbird which was done.

To those who have studied them even superficially, it is readily apparent that known heraldic screens fall into two categories: those that were true partitions and had circular or oval entrances through the center and those that were merely rearwall decorations. The first occupied the space between the rear house pillars and served to partition off the chief's sleeping apartment. This was no doubt the type that Emmons had in mind when he wrote Paalen that they were to be found in only half a dozen chief's houses in Southeastern Alaska.

The second type was a poor imitation of the other, regarded by the occupants of the house as heraldic but in most cases a late development for installation in modern framed houses. Most of them date from around 1900.

At first glance one might get the impression that there was a gradual transition from the one type to the other but this was probably not the case. The artistic flowering or renaissance of the art of the Northwest Coast between 1830 and 1880 or thereabouts, took place as a result of the accumulation of wealth derived from the sea otter trade. This produced the fine community houses and the elaborate totem poles which either were unknown before or were possessed by only a few great chiefs on the coast prior to 1830. It was in this period that the Rainwall was produced. The Bear Screen of the Wrangell Tlingit must have been produced after the Russians established themselves there in 1834. The Chief Shakes community house contained the house posts of an earlier *Shark House* at Kotslitan and if this house had possessed a screen it is certain that it, too, would have been brought to Wrangell to take its honored place between the rear house pillars. Instead, however, the Bear Screen was made and set up between the Shark Pillars to honor another of Chief Shakes's many perogatives, the Bear that in legend had led the clan to mountain-top safety during the flood.

After the decline of the fur trade on the Northwest Coast due to depletion of the sea otter and other factors including the purchase of Alaska by the United States, stagnation set in the areas occupied by the Tlingit and Haida, and native art and culture suffered a set-back from which it never recovered. However, beginning in the 1880's with the discovery of gold at Juneau, the Indians found employment at wages for the first time as miners, loggers and packers. Savings from wages found their way into clan coffers and the chiefs once again were provided with the affluence necessary for one more short-lived cultural binge around the turn of the century. Indian communities in the white man's towns of Juneau, Sitka, Skagway, Wrangell, and Ketchikan and in their own villages of Klukwan, Yindustucky, Angoon, Kake, and Hoonah, together with some of the Kaigani Haida villages suddenly began to put up large framed community houses embellished with fretwork and lathe-turned posts and fences. Ornate dead houses were built and much money was spent on funerals, potlatches and ceremonial visits. These events are fairly well documented in the newspapers of the time and in photographs taken by pioneer photographers of the area. Even some totem poles were erected after 1900 at Ketchikan, Wrangell and Kake but they were poor imitations of those erected prior to 1880 since the professional expert artisans had grown too old to work or had died off and virtually none had been trained to take their places.

The heraldic screens of this era were in general made of boards cut in local sawmills. The *Thunderbird Screen* of Yakutat, now in the Alaska State Museum, was made in Juneau in 1905 at a cost of $400.00. The *Kadjuk Screen* of Yakutat, also in the State Museum was painted by Sitka Jack in Sitka at about the same time. Both of these screens show the characteristic art of the Chilkat blanket pattern board. The Reverend Livingston Jones, longtime early Alaska missionary had this to say about a screen still to be seen in the Auke Indian village section of Juneau, "A few years ago an audacious native of the Auk village at Juneau had the grampus elaborately painted on the inside of the back wall of his house. This little piece of art originally cost him six hundred dollars, but before he was through with it, it cost him much more. A terrible commotion followed, as he was not entitled to use the *Keet* (killer whale or grampus) as his crest. The row was on for a long time, and the affair was finally settled by a money payment."

In an album of photographs taken by Vincent Sobolef principally at Angoon and Killisnoo about 1906 there is a picture of a very fine heraldic screen complete with entrance hole that must have once graced the rear wall of a community house. It is photographed against the papered wall of a frame house. The central figure appears to be the Gonakadet and the whole composition is reminiscent of a Chilkat blanket pattern board. The screen appears to have been very old in 1906.

The Museum of Modern Art in its "Indian Art of the United States" figures on page 175 a painted partition from a Nootka house, collected about 1929 by Emmons. It and its mate are also figured by Inverarity (plates 10 & 11). It is stated that the screen was made on Vancouver Island about 1850. It is painted on adzed boards fastened together with root fiber, a common method of joining boards all along the coast before nails appeared. However, it does not look as old as claimed. The lightning snake, wolf, thunderbird and whale are featured. The legend describes the whale as a *killer whale* although no teeth are shown and the dorsal fin is wrong. From the form of the dorsal fin it would appear that a *little piked whale* was intended. All figures are stylized in a manner roughly resembling Northwest Coast art. The authors opine that "painting is almost certainly an older art on the Northwest Coast than sculpture for which the region is so famed."

Mackenzie (1801) in describing an Indian house that he saw on the Northwest Coast in 1793 at about 52 degrees north latitude made this statement (p. 331) "The posts, poles, and figures, were

painted red and black but the sculpture of these people is superior to their painting." This has always been my observation although some of the artists, particularly those who painted the designs on the chief's woven spruceroot hats had approached virtuosity in their art. But since on this coast a useful article always precedes the decoration there can be little doubt that sculpture came first in this woodworking culture.

The center of all things cultural and artistic on the Northwest Coast at the time of discovery was in the region of the Queen Charlotte Islands and the adjacent mainland occupied respectively by Haida and Tsimshian. This is a region of giant red cedar trees which provided a wood so soft and easily worked that massive houses, huge war canoes, and gigantic columns could be made from it with simple tools. Although apparently scarce, it is significant that heraldic poles and house pillars were reported from the first, and long before anyone saw a heraldic screen. Beyond the range of the red cedar, that is, north of Wrangell, the various tall monuments of red cedar disappear. Both early explorers and later travelers and scholars agree that totem poles were not in use there, at least until around the turn of the century. Krause (1885) who was in Klukwan and other villages of the Panhandle in 1881-82 says this (page 88) "We saw a different type of gable in an old house of the Killisnoo at Angoon where the triangular gable space was raised and painted with bright, partly effaced mineral pigments. Langsdorf also mentions a similarly painted gable (page 89). Among the Chilkat only one totem pole was found, in the form of two whales lying on top of each other, which was repeated on both sides of a house in Klukwan, belonging to the chief of the whale clan. Likewise, only one totem was found at Gaudekan, the village of the Huna. It was of medium size and looked new, as though it had been recently erected. The Sitka and the Killisnoo had no poles at all, but a large number were seen in the Stikine settlement near Wrangell where they attained considerable height."

Niblack is silent on Heraldic screens although he discusses houses and mentions painted house fronts (Niblack 1890, p. 306) In plate LXVII he shows the body of Chief Skowl of Kasaan lying in state at the rear of his house surrounded by his personal effects and the tokens of his wealth (winter of 1882-83). The space between the rear house pillars is significantly bare.

Louis and Florence Shotridge, a Chilkat couple, writing in the University of Pennsylvania Museum Journal of September 1913, in their figure 83 show

HOONAH. The Tlingit residents of this little village didn't go in for heraldic totem poles in front of their houses. Instead, they had painted compositions similar to indoor heraldic screens that served the same purpose. There were, however, short memorial poles in their cemetery on an islet across the way.

Case & Draper.

screens and houseposts from the house of the chief family of the Kagwantons of Klukwan. The larger screen displays the *Grisly Bear* emblem and the smaller one, the *Killerwhale*. In writing about these screens, the authors state (p. 94) "In some houses, in the rear between the two carved posts, a screen is fitted, forming a kind of partition which is always carved and painted. Behind this screen is the chief's sleeping place. The smaller screens along the side walls are seldom decorated, as this is done only when a chief's nephew or brother has distinguished himself in war. . . ."

In accounting for the lack of exterior totem poles in the Chilkat villages, the Shotridges say this, "One often hears it said by the older people that originally totem poles were used inside of the houses only, to support the huge roof beams. The carvings and paintings on them were usually those of the family crests. These posts were regarded with respect very much as a flag is by a nation. Even when the Chilkats had acquired modern tools with which to make totem poles they did not fill their villages with tall poles like some other tribes, chiefly because they wanted to keep to the original idea. . . ."

In a communication from Wilson Duff, Curator of Anthropology at the Provincial Museum, Victoria, B.C. in answer to my inquiry relative to a "Wall Board" credited to that museum in Gunther's publication, "Indians of the Northwest Coast" (1951) he says, "We have very little information on our wallboard. It was collected in 1913 on the Nass River by Dr. C. F. Newcombe. He does not seen to have left any written account of it beyond the caption. "Tsimshian chief's carved crest board" on

the photograph published in our 1913 Annual Report. . . . We do not have any other carved screens of this type. I do not think they could have been at all common among the Tsimshian. They are not included in Dr. Barbeau's field notes when lists of chief's totem poles, houses, crest costumes and such are given." From the photograph, the central figure appears to be the Gonakadet. The border of faces is strongly reminiscent of the Rainwall. The panels making up the board are horizontal, laced with root fiber. The dimensions are 73″ × 67″.

Today, the known heraldic screens *in situ*, in museums, or in memory are from localities beyond the region of giant red cedar trees where heraldic columns were in use. The Rainwall is still in Klukwan, along with four or five others. Another at the University of Pennsylvania Museum came from there. There is still at least one in Yakutat (on a ceiling) and three in the State Museum that came from there. At least one remains in Sitka, another in the Juneau native village. There are photographs of one that was formerly in Angoon and another in Wrangell. There may be others for such heraldic devices in Tlingit possession have a habit of *going underground* for long periods and then coming to light to the amazement of even local residents who didn't know they existed. Then there are the Tsimshian and Nootka panels already discussed. From what evidence there is at hand, it seems reasonable to surmise that heraldic screens replaced heraldic columns in areas beyond the convenient range of giant red cedars and especially in the latter days.

If it has been sufficiently established that the

primitive forebear of the heraldic screen was the treasure chest front panel decoration, then it fits squarely into a pattern of action followed in the development of other art expressions of the area. It has been postulated (Keithahn '53) that the entire Northwest Coast art style came to this region intact, in portable form; that house pillars are large scale reproductions of heraldic charms or pendants; that totem poles are greatly enlarged replicas of chief's staffs; that the robes known as Chilkat blankets came from an earlier leathern shaman's apron; that the medicine box was patterned after a *soul catcher;* that even the chief's copper prototype was a copper arrowhead and ornate house facades were derived from low relief carved, painted and inlaid chest panels. This innate ability or propensity to take a small, easily portable object of decorative or plastic art and then, in an era of great affluence, to suddenly expand it into something entirely different in function is the secret of Northwest Coast artisanship. This is the reason why this art style blossomed so suddenly during the sea otter hunting days that we have been unable to recognize its humble beginnings. This is why it declined so sharply as the sea otter disappeared, then flared up briefly in the next generation after gold was discovered at Juneau and in the Klondike when Indians became wage earners. For the ethnologist this may be the final answer as to whether this outstanding art style is indiginous or derivitive. And because it has blossomed twice since the coming of Europeans to this coast, is it too much to hope that it may bloom once again?

HAIDA HOUSES IN UNIVERSITY OF BRITISH COLUMBIA TOTEM PARK, VANCOUVER, B.C. Here are seen replicas of two Haida Mortuaries in the foreground. Heraldic Poles stand before each house. In early houses the entrance was through a portal in the base of the pole.
Photo by Courtesy of Dr. Stanley Read.

TOTEM OF CHIEF ANNAHOOTS — SITKA ALASKA   CASE & DRAPER

WOLF MOTIF FALSE HOUSE PILLARS. The Wolf is the totem of the Kag-wan-ton Clan of Tlingits. Although known through the Tlingit nation as a warrior clan coming from the Interior their chief, Annahoots, was friendly to the Russians. Pillars like these were introduced in recent times for heraldic and decorative use in frame buildings where house pillars were of no further functional use.

Photo taken in Sitka by Case and Draper circa 1904.

Chapter Fourteen

LEGENDS IN CEDAR

The Gonakadet (Old Witch Totem Pole)

Next to *Raven*, the most popular subject for totem pole decoration was the *Gonakadet*. Known also to the Haida as *Wasgo*, this lake monster is generally depicted as an aquatic wolf with some of the features of the killerwhale. The Haida often depict it with a duck-like beak and one story about it says its head was like a house.

There are several Gonakadet stories but the most popular one concerns a high-born young man who was having mother-in-law trouble. Being the wife of a chief and used to having her own way, this woman seems to have despised him because he resisted her domination, and especially was she irked by his gambling. After each meal she would order every bit of food put out of sight so that there would be nothing left for him to eat when he came home from his gambling. Then she would order the slaves to put out the fire so that he would be unable to cook anything for himself. When he would come into the community house long after dark, the woman would remark, sarcastically, "My fine son-in-law has been cutting wood for me." A similar remark would be flung at him at every opportunity.

Although the young man had a kind and loving wife, he found that he could not endure her mother's constant nagging forever. At some distance behind the village there was a lake in which the monster Gonakadet was reputed to dwell. There at the lakeside he built himself a small cedar cabin where he lived alone. But he was not idle there; his intention was to study the monster and then devise a means to trap it. As his plans matured he felled a tall cedar tree so that its tip was in the water. Then he carefully stripped it of its branches and peeled off the bark. With fire-hardened wedges and a stone maul he split the tree nearly to the butt. Next he inserted crosspieces which sprung the two halves of the tree wide apart and held them there at great tension.

When summer came and the villagers left for the fishing grounds, the young man went with them and caught many salmon. These he brought back to his cabin and with them baited his trap. By letting the bright red salmon down into the water on a line, he finally lured the Gonakadet into the space between the sprung tree-halves whereupon he knocked out the trigger and the monster was trapped. For many hours it thrashed about trying to free itself. At times it dragged the tree completely under the water. But eventually, unable to get loose, it gave up the struggle and died.

Then the young man removed the Gonakadet from the trap, skinned it carefully and placed

139

Base of Yax-te totem pole figured on page 141. See story.
Photo by author.

the hide on a stretcher for drying. When it was cured, the young man got into the skin and walked into the water. As he had hoped, dressed in the hide, he had all of the powers of the Gonakadet, itself. He explored the lake bottom, finding there a beautiful house which had been the monster's home.

The secret of his good fortune he kept from everybody except his wife and she was charged to reveal it to no one.

After a long hard winter, early spring found all of the people's dried salmon used up and the villagers were faced with the threat of famine. Then the young man put on his Gonakadet skin and swam in the sea every night. Only his wife knew of his activities and only to her did he reveal the supernatural aspects of his new power. "I will be back each morning before the raven calls," he said, "but if the raven calls before I return, do not look for me for I shall be dead in this life."

That night he caught a salmon and before the raven called, he brought it to the village and laid in on the sand before his mother-in-law's door. Rising early the next morning this woman spied the salmon and concluded that the tide had dropped it there. According to custom, the hungry villagers were invited to share it.

The following night the young man caught two salmon and left them in the same place. When his mother-in-law found these she was overjoyed and wondered what it was that was bringing her this good fortune. "It must be a spirit," she thought.

The young man now slept more than ever during the day, being tired from swimming about all night in search of salmon. His mother-in-law would berate him soundly, saying, "Imagine men sleeping all day when there is a famine. If it were not for me going around picking up fish the whole village would starve!" His wife who knew who was providing the salmon said nothing.

The next morning the woman found a halibut before her door, and sensing a rhythm in the strange happenings predicted that two halibut would be there on the morrow. The young man, hearing her prediction, fulfilled it by catching two halibut. Then she told her husband, the chief, to forbid anyone to go out on the beach until she had been there, giving as her reason that she had had a vision. Of course, she wished only to make sure that she should get full credit for everything that was found there. Then she predicted that she would find a seal and as she had foretold, a seal was there in the morning. The hair was singed off, the skin scrubbed white and the seal cooked whole for the benefit of the community.

People now began to regard her as a great shaman and she did everything in her power to encourage such belief. She ordered a claw headdress made such as shaman's wear and a rattle and an apron decorated with puffin's beaks, and a mask which she named *Food-Finding Spirit*. She began to talk continually about her spirits, and sang songs about their power. High caste people paid much attention to her and praised her spirits. Popularity made her still more cruel to her son-in-law and

140

she now spoke of him derisively as the *Sleeping Man.*

As time went on she called successively for two seals, then one sea lion, two sea lions, one whale. Now she was selling food to the villages and had so much food stored away in boxes that the people were awed by her great wealth.

Each night the task had been getting greater for the young man and this time he had barely gotten in with the whale before the raven called. To his wife he cautioned, "Do not take any of that food unless she offers it." And then he added, "If I am found dead in this skin, put me along with the skin in the place where I used to hide it, and you will get help."

Then the day came when the pseudo-shaman called for two wales. The young man caught them but to bring them in exceeded the strength even of the Gonakadet. All night long he struggled to get them ashore but just as he reached the beach the raven called and he fell dead.

The mother-in-law went out as usual and found the two whales with a strange monster lying dead between them. All the villagers came down to the beach to see it. It had claws that shone like burnished copper and a big wolf-like head with long upright ears. Two great fins stood up on its back and it had a long curling tail. The simple villagers thought it must be the food-finding spirit.

Just then they heard someone crying, and upon looking in that direction saw the chief's daughter approaching weeping bitterly. "Why does the chief's daughter call that monster her husband?" they asked each other.

When the young woman reached the shore she turned to her mother angrily, saying, "Where are your spirits now? You lied! You said you had spirits when you actually had none. That is why this has happened to my husband."

Everyone in the village now crowded about. "Mother, is this your Food-Finding Spirit? Why did your spirit die? Real spirits never die. If this is your spirit bring it to life again."

Then the girl requested the help of someone who was spiritually clean and they opened the monster's mouth revealing the body of her husband. "He must have been killed by that monster," said the villagers.

When the young woman and her helpers went to the lake to deposit the body according to the dead man's instructions they saw for the first time the trap that had caught the Gonakadet and the tools the young man had used to make it. For the first time they knew the truth. All the villagers then went to the lake to see it for themselves and to pay their respects to the man who had saved them from starvation. That is, all except the mother-in-law. Her shame was now more than she could bear and she died in convulsions, bloody froth coming from her mouth.

Every evening thereafter the bereaved young woman went to the tree where her husband's body lay and wept. But one evening she perceived a ripple on the waters of the lake and then she saw the Gonakadet rise. Speaking in her husband's voice it called her to it. Then it said, "Get on my back and

YAX-TE TOTEM POLE AT AUKE VILLAGE SITE (two views). Erected in 1941 to mark the site of old Auke Village 16 miles north of Juneau on Glacier Highway, this is the only totem pole showing *Yax-te*, the "Big Dipper" constellation which was the clan symbol of the Auke Tlingit. It is significant that these Indians represent *Ursa Major* (great she-bear) as a bear-like creature as did the Romans, Greeks, and other ancients. (See story)   Photo by author.

Goo-Teekhl, the Cannibal Giant

Many years ago there dwelt in the forest north of Klukwan, a cannibal so huge that he was the terror of all the Chilkat country. Said to be sixteen feet tall, more powerful than a grisly bear, and of voracious appetite, this wild man would rush out of the woods, strip the salmon from the people's drying racks, gobble it up, then retreat to the fastnesses of the forest. Warriors sent against him were invariably killed and eaten, for their arrows and spears could not pierce his thick hide. Frequent incursions of this cannibal against the Chilkat Indians and their stores of winter food threatened the very existence of this tribe. Something had to be done or the entire village would be exterminated.

Eventually it fell to the people of the *Ganaxadi* clan who dwelt in the *Frog House* to take steps that were to free them from the scourge of the forest. Members of this clan searched for the home of the cannibal until they came upon a huge house deep in the timber. Red smoke was billowing from the smoke hole, and taking this to be the sign of the cannibal they prepared to deal with him there. As soon as it was dark they dug a deep pit such as the ones they dug to trap grisly bears. Near the bottom of the pit they set a large net made from bear sinew, strong and elastic. Then the pit was covered over with light poles, branches, grass and litter until it looked as natural as the forest floor.

When daylight came, one of the Indians made an appearance in front of the house. Goo-teekhl, seeing him, took after him, expecting to capture him for his breakfast. The Indian ran across the pit but the cannibal, because of his great weight, crashed into the hole and became entangled in the meshes of the net where he soon lay helpless on his back.

Seeing that he could not escape, the Frog House people began heaping dried leaves and sticks upon their enemy with the idea of burning him in the pit. Understanding their intentions, Goo-teekhl called to them, saying, "Foolish men. You think that you can burn me up. Know then that I am a supernatural being. Even though you burn me, I will continue to eat your people throughout the years and for all time!"

But the people were desperate, so in spite of the warning, they started the fire. For four days and nights the fire was kept burning fiercely. Not a vestige of the cannibal remained. But just to be sure that he was entirely consumed, the Indians took long poles and stirred among the hot coals at the bottom of the pit. Then an unaccountable thing happened. As the multitude of fiery sparks spiralled out of the pit and up into the air, they

TOTEM OF THE CANNIBAL GIANT "GOO-TEEKHL." When this cannibal was captured and burned to death his thirst for blood was transmitted to mosquitoes that were created from the hot sparks rising from his funeral pyre. The image is fed daily and on all ceremonial occasions in the belief that fortune smiles on those who dream of Goo-teekhl and recognize his power and immortality. Totem and Frog pillar at right may be seen at Klukwan.
Photo by Lloyd V. Winter taken in 1893.

hold on tight." She did so and down beneath the waves they plunged together.

People say they still live there in a beautiful house and that their numerous children are known as "Daughters of the Creek." They reside at the head of every stream and to see them or either of their spirit parents will surely bring one good luck.

* * *

142

suddenly took the form of swarms of mosquitos that immediately attacked the people with fury, biting through their skins and sucking their blood. Goo-teekhl had made good his threat!

In order to appease the cannibal the people of the Frog House went back to their villages and carved a great image of Goo-teekhl which may still be seen in their house in Klukwan. Every day this totem is fed; oil is poured in its mouth, flour is sifted on its body; sometimes a medicine man makes medicine before it. They still hope that someday Goo-teekhl will relent and when he does, mosquitos will no longer bite.

* * *

The Story of Duk-toothl or Ka-ha-si

In old Tuxekan, the ancient home of the Klawock people, dwelt *Gal-wet*, a chief of the *Tak-wan-edi* or "Winter People." Every day he bathed in the sea for strength, and his people bathed with him. In the cold, gray winter mornings he would rise, run down to the sea, and rush in followed by the members of his clan. Then they would whip each other with switches until their blood ran hot. After that they would go to a certain tree which the chief would try to twist from top to bottom. Or he would go to another from which he would try to pull out a branch. He was testing his strength in preparation for an expedition against the sea lions.

Galwet had a nephew and heir who was a great disappointment to the entire village. He was weak and cowardly and would lie abed when all the others were bathing for strength. They called him *Duk-toothl* or "Black Skin" because he never bathed and was blackened with soot from sleeping too close

THE CHIEF SKOWL TOTEM POLE. This elaborate monument which so plainly shows European influence was erected by the great Haida chief, Skowl, at Kasaan in the early 80's and has since been removed to Ketchikan where it may be seen in the city park. It was ordered carved to commemorate the baptism of the chief and his family in the Greco-Russian Church at New Archangel (Sitka). The unusual art style is derived from that on cards picturing saints, cherubs etc., given to Skowl by the Russian bishop.

The eagle surmounting the pole is Chief Skowl's totem; beneath it is the figure of a Russian saint; the third figure, apparently emerging from clouds, is the face of the Archangel Michael, and beneath it the Russian bishop. Next comes another eagle, beneath which is a figure of Skowl's son-in-law, Vincent Baronovich, an Austrian by birth, hailing from Trieste, Dalmatia. Baronovich was an English subject and together with Skowl, held in contempt the "Yankee Government" so it is unlikely the lower eagle represents the United States which had recently purchased Alaska. Skowl's daughter, Mrs. Vincent Baronovich, largely financed the carving and it was no doubt for her sake that her husband's figure was included. He died in 1879 and Skowl in the winter of 1882-83.

Photo by Schallerer.

to the fire. One day, however, his aunt took him in hand secretly and told him how he was disgracing his clan and that they would lose caste when he became chief. He promised her that he would make himself strong and worthy of the respect normally accorded a chief.

But Duk-toothl continued to feign weakness, and though he continued to lie abed when the others bathed, at night after all the rest were asleep, he would steal off and do the same things the others did, for hours at a time. He would remain in the icy water so long that he would sometimes float in order to rest his feet. On coming out of the water he would throw water on the ashes of the fire so as to make it steam, then lay his mat on top. That was the only bed he had. The people continued to think of him as a low, dirty fellow, but in reality he kept himself pure and would not lie or steal. He did not say a word when they made fun of him, although he was already strong enough to have thrashed any of them had he so desired. When they sent him after big pieces of firewood he acted as if they were very hard to lift, but they believed he was just lazy so would give him very little to eat.

The hunters went on in this way, bathing every day with their chief, while *Black-skin* secretly bathed at night. After they were through bathing and testing their strength, the hunters would make a big fire, take their breakfast and then go after wood.

One night, while Duk-toothl was bathing, he heard a whistle which sounded to him like that of of a loon. He thought, "Now that I have been seen, I had better let myself go." So we went toward the place where the sound came from. There he saw a short, thick-set man standing on the beach clothed in a bearskin. The stranger rushed towards him, picked him up bodily and threw him to the ground. Then he said, "You can't do it yet. Don't tell anyone about me. I am *Strength*. I have come to help you." Toward morning *Black-skin* came in feeling very happy for he thought that he had had an important experience. He kept thinking of Strength all the time. He could not forget him but he was quieter than ever in his manner. When they were playing in the house he would pay no attention, and if they said mean things to him, he let them go unnoticed. He took abuse that would never have been tolerated by a member of the chief's family and served the warriors as if he were their slave.

In olden times the boys would wrestle in the chief's house while their elders looked on, and they would try to get Black-skin to wrestle, too. Sometimes the little boys would wrestle him, and he would let them throw him. Then they would make fun of him saying, "The idea of a great big man like you being thrown by a child."

The next time he went bathing, Black-skin felt very happy for now he knew that he had strength. Anything that had been hard for him to do now was easy. That night he heard the whistle again. He looked around and saw the same short, thick-set man who said, "Come over this way. Come over to me." Then they seized one another, and as soon as the short man felt Black-skin's grip, he said, "Don't throw me down. Now you have strength. You are not to go into the water again. Go from here right up to that tree and try to pull the limb out." Duk-toothl did as ordered and found that he could pull out the branch easily. Then he put it back again. After he had passed this test, the man told him to go to the other tree. "Twist it right down to the roots," he said. So Black-skin did. And then he untwisted it so that it looked as it did before.

Just after he got to bed the hunters got up to go bathing. As they passed him, the boys would pull his hair, saying, "Come on and go in bathing, too," but he paid no attention making believe that he was asleep.

After the men had bathed they went up to the limb as usual to see if they were strong enough for the sealion hunt. This time, Galwet pulled it out with ease. Black-skin lay in bed listening to the shouting they made over this great feat. Then Galwet ran to the other tree and twisted it down to its roots. When the party came back to the house, they told the story again and again, "Galwet pulled out that limb! Galwet twisted the tree to its roots!" The chief himself felt very proud, and the people of the village were happy that he had done so, especially his two wives. Then they tried to get Black-skin out of bed. They laughed at him, saying "Your chief has pulled out the limb. Why couldn't you? He has also twisted that tree. You sleep like a chief and let your chief go bathing in the morning." They laughed at him, saying, "He is sleeping this morning because he has pulled out that limb and twisted that tree."

Since they had been bathing in order to gain strength to hunt the sealions, they now felt that they were ready to go. Then one of the young hunters said, "To-morrow we are going after sealions. I wonder which part of the canoe Black-skin will sleep in. He is such a powerful fellow." And another boy said, "Why, this Black-skin will sit in the bow of the canoe so that he can land first. He will tear the sealions in two." Duk-toothl listened to all of this abuse but paid no attention to it.

People of the town spent the whole day going

KWAKIUTL THUNDERBIRD TOTEMS. In front of Indian homes at Alert Bay, B.C.

Photo by author.

to the place where the limb had been pulled out and the tree twisted off. This was an important event to them for it meant a party would soon be going after sealions. These people practically lived on sealion meat and it was hard to get. Because of the danger, only the strongest of the men who had been bathing with the chief were allowed to go out to the sealion rocks to hunt them.

The elder of the chief's two wives had taken pity on Black-skin, and would do little favors for him when no one was watching. So after Black-skin had bathed secretly he came to this aunt and said, "Will you give me a clean shirt? It doesn't matter much what it is so long as it is clean, and something for my hair."

"Are you asked to go?" queried the aunt.
"I am not asked," he replied, "but I am going." So she prepared food for him to take along and put it in as small a package as she could.

When the sealion hunters began to embark in their big dugout canoe, Black-skin came down, too, but they all began to shout, "Don't let him come! Don't let him come!"

Seeing that he was determined to get in, they began pushing the canoe out as fast as they could. Black-skin then seized the canoe and they struck his fingers to make him let go. It sounded like beating on a board, his fingers were so hard. But with all of them shoving it out, he exerted very little of his strength to pull the canoe back, then jumped in. Then the hunters talked very mean to him, but the chief said, "Oh, let him be. He will bail out the canoe for us on the way over." So he sat in the place where one bails.

The chief might have suspected something after his nephew pulled the canoe back against the entire crew but he did not let his manner show it. The hunters continued to ridicule the nephew. "Black-skin came along to tear the sealions in two," said one. "How many sealions shall I skin for you?" asked another. Black-skin said nothing.

The sealion rocks had very precipitous and slippery sides against which the great waves broke, so Galwet waited until the canoe was lifted upon the crest of a wave, then jumped ashore. He was a very powerful man, and seizing a small sealion by the

tail, he smashed its head to pieces on the rocks. Then he thought he would do the same thing to a large one. These huge bull sealions are called *men-of-the-islands*. He went up to the very largest of these and sat astride of his tail, intending to tear it in two, but the big bull threw him up into the air. When the uncle came down he was smashed to death on the rocks.

Now, when Black-skin saw what had happened to his uncle, he felt bad. Putting his hand into his bundle of clothes, he took out and put on his hair ornament and his clean shirt while all were watching him. Then he said, "I am the one that pulled out that limb, and I am the man who twisted that tree." He spoke in a polite form that high caste Indians used in those days, and all listened to him in awe.

Now he said, "Take the canoe closer to the rock." When they did so he started walking forward, stepping on the seats which broke under his weight, precipitating their occupants to the bottom of the canoe. The young men who were sitting in his way, he threw back as if they had been small birds. Then the hunters were frightened, being afraid that he would take revenge on them for what they had done to him in the past. But he only jumped ashore where his uncle had gone, and walked straight up, the slippery cliff. The smaller sealions in his way he killed simply by hitting them on the head with his fist or by stepping on them. He was looking only at the big bull that had killed his uncle, for he did not want it to get away. When he finally reached it he grasped it by the hind flukes and tore it in two.

After he had killed all the sealions left on the rock he loaded the canoe with them so that they could be taken back to the village for food. But before he could get into the boat, his companions shoved off, leaving him stranded. When they got back to the village they told their townsmen what had happened. When they told them that it was Black-skin who had pulled the branch out of the tree and had twisted the tree off they were very

THE "OLD WITCH" TOTEM POLE. This fine Haida pole originally stood at old Sukkwan, a Haida village off the West Coast of Prince of Wales Island, near Hydaburg. The "Old Witch" was in reality a pseudo-shamaness and the story is a Haida version of the Tlingit "Gonakadet" story, a legend of "mother-in-law" trouble. The pole was purchased many years ago from the original Haida owners by Dr. Robert Simpson of Juneau and is shown in this view in front of the old Nugget Shop on Franklin Street. When the present Nugget Shop was erected on Seward Street, Dr. Simpson presented the pole to the city of Juneau and it now may be seen beside the city library.

Photo by author.

troubled. "Why did you leave him out there?" they asked. "Why didn't you bring him in?"

Left alone on the rocks, Black-skin didn't know what would happen to him. He had nothing to use to make a fire and no way to escape. So he dressed the sea lions that he had killed and had not loaded in the canoe, then carefully prepared their intestines for drying. After that, there being nothing else he could do, he lay down and went to sleep, his head covered with his blanket. Presently he heard something that sounded like the beating of sticks. Then he heard someone say, "I have come after you." He looked around, but could see nothing except a black duck that was swimming about in front of him. When he saw that the duck was coming toward him he said to it, "I have seen you already," and the duck answered, "I am sent after you. Get on my back but keep your eyes closed tight."

Black-skin closed his eyes and presently the duck said, "Now, open your eyes." He opened them and saw that he was in a fine house. It was the house of the sealions. It is through this story that the natives to this day say that everything is like a human being. Each kind of animal has its "way of living." Why do fish die when taken out of water? It is because they have a "way of living" of their own down there.

Meanwhile the elder wife of the chief who had helped Black-skin was mourning for her husband and nephew. Her husband's body was still on the sealion rocks. The older people were also saying to the hunters who had left him, "Why did you do it? A powerful fellow like that it scarce. We want such a man among us."

Then the widow begged the young men to go back to the island and bring home her nephew and her husband's body but the younger wife didn't care either way. Finally, a party was gotten together who went out to the place where they found the chief's body but could not find Black-skin. So they took the body aboard, loaded the canoe with the carcasses of sealions, and went back to the village.

When the older people heard that Black-skin was missing, they all said that something was wrong. They asked the shaman to find out what it was and when he had made medicine he told them that Black-skin was not dead and that they would see him again. He said that he was off with some kind of wild animal.

This information troubled the villagers a great deal. They felt bad to think that he had behaved so lowly before low-caste people, and now feared that he was suffering somewhere again when he might just as well have rightfully occupied his uncle's place.

Black-skin was living with the sealion people who looked like ordinary people to him, although he knew who they really were. One of the boys in their house was crying all the time, apparently in great pain. But the sealion people could not see what ailed him. Black-skin could see that he had a barbed spear point in his side. Then one of the sealions said, "That shaman there knows what is the matter. He is saying, 'How is it that they cannot see the bone in the side of that child?'"

Then Black-skin said, "I am not a shaman, but I can take it out." So, taking out his skinning knife, he carefully cut the bone spear out. Then, calling for warm water, he washed out the festering wound and dressed it the best he could. The boy recovered rapidly and because he was high caste, his people

THE ONE-LEGGED FISHERMAN POLE. This memorial was erected by Kudanake (Shakes VII) in memory of his uncle, "Kauk-ish" who died in 1897 leaving him property. An earlier pole in the same design was sketched at Kotslitan in 1879 by John Muir, but has fallen.

Photo by the author.

said to Black-skin, "You have saved our prince's life. You may have anything that any of us possesses."

There was only one thing that Black-skin wanted, a box that hung in the rafters overhead. This box was a kind of medicine to bring any kind of wind that was wanted. The sealions would push the box up and down on the water, calling the wind to it like a dog, whistling and saying, "Come to this box. Come to this box." That is why the natives whistle for the winds and call them up like dogs.

The sealion people told Black-skin to get into the box and as soon as he did so, he saw that he was far out to sea. He then began to call for the wind that blows shoreward, and it carried him ashore. Then he got out of the box and hung it out on the limb of a tree in a sheltered place. He did this because the sealion people had told him to take good care of the box and not to go near anything unclean with it.

Black-skin had landed only a short distance from his own village, so he walked home, wearing a wreath of braided sealion intestines on his head. His aunt was very glad to see him, feeling just the same as though her husband had come home. Then he asked all of the townspeople to assemble, and those who had been cruel to him and had abandoned him on the rocks were very much ashamed. Some were so frightened when he came back that they fled into the forest. But he thought, "If I had not made myself so humble, they might not have treated me that way." So he overlooked their cruelty, saying, "Some of you know how cruel you were to me. Now you are ashamed of yourselves. But some of you feel good because you always felt kindly towards me. It will always be so hereafter, that people who are cruel to poor and weak people will be ashamed of it afterwards. So do not make fun of poor people again as you did when my uncle was alive."

After this day, Black face was known no longer by his nickname but by his true name, Ka-ha-si.

* * *

The Kwakiutl Thunderbird Totem Pole

No totem pole on the Northwest Coast enjoys so much popularity as the Nimpkish Kwakiutl Thunderbird pole which for years dominated the totem pole cluster at Alert Bay, B.C. Because of its beautifully-designed outspread wings and its gay, contrasting colors, it has been selected to illustrate travel folders and magazine or book illustrations in preference to any other totem pole for many years. Souvenir totem poles in gold, silver, bone, ivory and wood are made in its design not only in Canada but in Alaska, Mexico, Switzerland and Japan as well.

The figures on this pole consist of Thunderbird with outspread wings at the top, perched upon the head of a ferocious grisly bear. The bear generally holds a slave in its paws but often only the slave's head is carved, beneath which is a chief's *copper* in the conventional shield shape. A story suggested by these figures and adapted from one of several versions follows.

In the dim, prehistoric past of the fogbound land of the Nimpkish Kwakiutl Indians, the people still dwelt in a deeper fog of ignorance and superstition. Without human knowledge and lacking the instincts of animals they were the most wretched of God's creatures.

So it came to pass that *Thunderbird*, looking down from his abode on high, saw mankind in all its misery. Having compassion, he decided to descend to earth to teach men the way they were expected to live.

Flying down to the earth below and assuming the form of a man, he selected a promising spot in a berrypatch beside a salmon-filled river. There he began constructing a large community house from the huge cedar logs which he made from trees he felled in the surrounding forest.

The house was made spacious and strong of hewed timbers and planks. Then he decorated it inside and out with carved and painted figures and designs of great beauty. He made hunting and fishing equipment such as bows, arrows, hooks, harpoons and nets out of the materials at hand. Also he made household furnishings such as chests, bowls and dishes of wood. He made baskets of spruceroot and mats of cedar bark. Then he caught and smoked many salmon and rendered candlefish and stored the oil in tight bentwood boxes. Berries were gathered and dried for winter use, and he pressed seaweed into cakes. All this food he stored away in boxes tied up with cedar bark rope which he made himself.

All summer Thunderbird, with the help of his personal servant, labored to produce this vast wealth and when it was at last assembled he took a grisly bear and commanded it to guard his possessions. He was now ready for the *social season* which always follows the *salmon season* on this coast. So he rested, and patiently awaited a visit from men who dwelt in the neighborhood.

Sometime later, as Thunderbird had anticipated, a band of natives drifting by in their crude hollowed log saw the wonderous house and paused awe-stricken at the sight. Thunderbird went down to the river's edge and invited the travellers to be his guests. Then he took them around and showed them in great detail just what everything was, how it was made and what it was for. After they had seen all of the things he had made he set a great feast before them and explained how it had been gathered and prepared for storage and for the table. It was the finest food any of the natives had ever tasted. After the dinner, Thunderbird asked them to return to their homes and follow his instructions and example thereafter.

But when the guests started to leave, they began taking Thunderbird's property with them. He vainly tried to explain the laws of private property to them but they would not listen. They sacked up everything that was movable and ended by taking him with them as a prisoner.

They had not gone far when a great storm came up suddenly. Soon the waves were running mountain high and rain poured down in sheets. Then from the coal-black clouds lightning began to flash and thunder rolled about the fleeing party.

Now on the verge of capsizing, the natives began throwing their loot overboard. They were about to throw their captive into the river when one of them chanced to notice that with each clap of thunder, their prisoner's eyes flashed like fire. It was then that they realized for the first time that there was a connection between their thievery and their present predicament. Suddenly they were aware that their hostage was none other than their principal god, Thunderbird, in disguise. Thereupon they promised that if Thunderbird would spare their lives they would follow his teachings forever.

The erring Indians were forgiven and immediately the wind died out, the sea became calm and the sun again shone forth from a cloudless sky. Thunderbird was thereupon returned to his house with his possessions and the natives departed, vowing to spread his instruction among all their tribes.

Thunderbird liked the country and decided to stay. In time he married the daughter of a nearby chief and this couple became the ancestors of all of the Nimpkish people under the Thunderbird totem. When the great benefactor died, his nephew succeeded him as chief and according to custom, erected a memorial to his famous uncle. This memorial was surmounted by Thunderbird with his wings outspread in a protecting attitude. Beneath him was the guardian of his property, Grisly Bear, who holds in his paws the slave or personal servant of Thunderbird. The slave holds a chief's copper, a shield-shaped symbol of wealth or property.

* * *

CHIEF JOHNSON'S POLE. The female figure at the base of this pole might well be the patron diety of Ketchikan for she is Fog Woman, creator of the salmon to which Ketchikan owes its prosperity.

U.S. Forest Service Photo.

The Stories on Chief Johnson's Totem Pole

This tall totem pole is quite likely the first one that a visitor will see upon reaching Alaska. It stands near the Federal Building in Ketchikan, at the junction of Mission and Stedman streets where it was set up in 1901 during a potlatch given by Chief Johnson, of the Kadjuk group of Tlingits. Surmounting the pole is *Kadjuk*, a mythological bird based on the golden eagle, a species rarely seen on the coast but common in the interior. As one of the fables concerning this bird goes, it amuses itself by dropping stones on unsuspecting ground hogs. If one is lucky enough to acquire one of these stones, his prosperity is assured for all time. Because of the extreme high caste of this bird, a great expanse of undecorated pole separates him from the more lowly creatures carved below. It may also symbolize Kadjuk's mountain habitat.

The twin bird forms appearing next are *Gitsanuk* and *Gitsaqeq,* the servants of Raven who appears beneath them with spreading wings. While these servants are actually ravens, they cannot be identified as such by their beaks, which in this instance are hooked. This is accounted for by the fact that Raven had previously sent them to get fire for the use of man on earth. In carrying the stolen embers in their beaks, the heat caused the beaks to melt as is shown in this carving.

The large female figure holding two salmon by their tails is *Fog Woman* who, in this episode of Raven's philandering life, is his wife. The figure may be recognized as female by the large labret worn in the lower lip. In the past, the Indian women of the Northwest Coast wore these decorations to show caste, and thereby gained the name *wooden-lipped people* from early navigators. They were never worn by the males.

The main story recalled at the base of this pole goes back to the days when there were no salmon, and Raven had to make out a miserable fare of cod, sculpins and an occasional halibut or herring. One day when Raven was encamped at Anan creek with his two slaves, they went out to midchannel to fish. Suddenly a heavy fog settled down, and he and his servants were lost; they could not even see beyond the bow of their canoe. Presently a beautiful woman materialized in the center of the canoe. She asked for Raven's spruceroot hat and upon receiving it, turned it upside down, whereupon the fog poured into it, leaving the sky clear again. Raven thereupon ordered his servants to paddle the canoe home, taking the woman with him. Raven fell in love with the woman of the fog and before long they were married.

One day when Raven was absent from his house, Fog Woman sent one of the slaves to get water in Raven's spruceroot hat. When he returned with the water, to his surprise, a bright shiny fish was swimming in the hat. This was the first salmon and Fog Woman bade the slave to cook it at once so that they might eat it before her husband returned.

When Raven came home he detected some fragments of red meat from the salmon on his slave's teeth and from him learned that Fog Woman had created the salmon. Upon inquiring how she did it, the woman told Raven he must first build a large smokehouse while she went up the creek to wash her hair. On the fourth day, he was to go look for salmon.

Following her instructions, Raven built a large smokehouse and on the fourth day, upon going to the bay early in the morning found it full of salmon. Fog Woman told him to look in the stream which he did, and found it, too, choked with salmon.

Now, together, Raven and his wife began the labor of catching, cleaning, smoking and drying, and storing a whole winter's supply of this precious fish. For the first time in his life, Raven felt rich and secure. It didn't take him long to forget that all this good fortune was due to his wife. Then he began to ignore and abuse her. He became mean and arrogant and daily his actions became more intolerable. His wife could do nothing to please him. Finally, in a fit of temper he struck her with a salmon's backbone and the sharp spines pierced her side. Deeply humiliated she left the house and started running toward the beach. Raven followed, trying to catch her but each time he reached for her she slipped through his fingers like mist. Then she seemed to drift out over the water, never to return.

Raven tried to reconcile his loss by the fact that he was now very wealthy and could easily get another wife so long as he was rich. But just then he heard a peculiar sound. Turning around, he was amazed to find that his great supply of dried salmon had suddenly come to life and were streaming down to the beach and swimming out to sea. Even his cache containing his winter's supply of smoked salmon was empty and only tracks leading toward the beach were left to show where his salmon had gone. Raven found himself as poor as before. But salmon had been created and have remained in Alaska to this day.

Some say that Fog Woman's daughters, the *Creek Women,* live at the head of every stream. It is the culminating joy of a salmon's life to fight its way to the headwaters of the stream for just one look at the *Woman of the Creek.* All of them die in the attempt save the steelhead, who by special dispensation, comes back year after year.

* * *

The One-legged Fisherman Totem Pole

The story related on this pole is one of the many adventures of *Kayak*, a mythological Tlingit hero. It was he who slew his father, *Lakishina*, a wolfish ancestor who delighted in killing his own children by sawing them to death on the spines of his red cod-skin coat. Kayak's mother had saved him from such a death, and also a brother and sister, by changing them into puppies whenever their father was home so that he would not recognize them. But by a strange curse, this sister was forbidden ever to look upon her brothers, on pain that if she did they would be turned to stone.

In this particular exploit, Kayak and his brother, learning that there was a fisherman at Yakutat who had a magic harpoon, journeyed thither in the hopes of obtaining it for his own use. The fisherman turned out to be a supernatural being of the eagle order except that it had only one leg. (The totem pole at Wrangell shows two, doubtless a concession to the dictates of Northwest Coast art which demands things to be in balance.) By means of this magic harpoon it secured salmon easily. Then it would string them on ropes and fly to its home in a grisly bear's den far up the creek.

The coat worn by the one-legged fisherman was ornamented by two bear's heads which, upon arriving home, would remove the salmon from the rope. One head would toss fish to a large male grisly bear and the other one would toss them to the female bear which was the one-legged fisherman's mother-in-law.

On the day following the one in which Kayak had observed all this, he dressed himself in the skin of a sea monster he had killed in an earlier adventure at Sitka, then hid under the water at the place where the salmon were schooled together. When the one-legged fisherman came down and threw his harpoon, Kayak grasped it. Then, cutting the line, he swam underwater with the coveted weapon until he could emerge from the water unseen. The one-legged fisherman dived for his lost harpoon-head repeatedly but finally had to give up trying to recover it.

Sometime later the fisherman caught Kayak with the magic harpoon in his hand and in the struggle to recover it, the one-legged fisherman was killed. Kayak thereupon skinned his opponent and got into the hide intending to deceive the fisherman's wife. But she detected the masquerade and together with her parents attacked Kayak. In the battle which ensued, all three grisly bears were killed and Kayak and his brother went on to more adventures.

After many harrowing escapades, none of which are recorded on the Wrangell pole, Kayak and his brother met their end while attempting to cross the Stikine river. The current was swift and their sister, apprehensive that they might be swept away, looked up at them whereupon both were instantly turned to stone. These stones are still pointed out to travellers on the Stikine river, not very far from Wrangell.

* * *

Origin of the Woodworm Emblem

Many years ago, among the natives of the Northwest Coast, it was the custom for high caste girls to be placed in seclusion for a period of several

RAVEN PILLAR and WOODWORM PILLAR. Two of the pillars still to be seen in the Whale House at Klukwan, Alaska. Photo from Emmons' The Whale House of the Chilkat.

PLATE 4.

months just prior to their reaching maturity. They were placed in a special apartment behind a painted heraldic screen and were forbidden to look at men or any of their hunting equipment for to do so would make the hunter unlucky.

Now it happened at old Tuxekan that a girl of the Ganaxadi clan while so confined picked up a woodworm that had been brought in on the firewood. Being very lonely she secretly made a pet of it. At first it would not eat anything she offered it and it appeared to be starving to death. Finally in desperation to save her pet she gave it her breast where it thereafter suckled like a child.

As time passed, the woodworm grew steadily and before long the girl had a difficult time keeping it out of sight. But at night when the girl and all the other villagers slept, the woodworm was busy making tunnels under the village. Then it would come up when people were asleep and eat their dried salmon and eulachon grease that they had put up for their winter stores.

One day the girl's mother, wondering how her daughter was occupying herself investigated her quarters and discovered the girl singing a lullaby to the woodworm which was now as big as a human being. Horrified, she called the Chief who took one look then immediately sent for the girl's uncle. Through a ruse they got the girl away from her quarters long enough to get a good look at the huge white monster which they found hidden behind the food storage boxes. Now they knew what it was that had been stealing their winter food supplies.

In order to protect the remainder of their supplies and rid their village of a much-feared monster, they decided to kill it. In secret preparation, the men made long wooden spears and fire-hardened the points. Then one day the girl's aunt sent for her. They were making the marten-skin robe she was to wear in the ceremony which would terminate her confinement and at which time she would be presented to the community as eligible for marriage.

As soon as the girl was out of the way, the men attacked the woodworm with their spears and killed it. Shortly thereafter the maid returned and seeing the dead woodworm, tearfully accused them of murdering her child. She could not be consoled and day after day and night after night she sang the woodworm lullaby until she died.

Because of this event the family of the girl took the woodworm as its crest and migrated northward, finally settling at Klukwan. There today in the Whale House one may still see the Woodworm house pillar, one of the finest remaining in Alaska. On it the girl is shown holding a woodworm while two others form her headdress. In the same house

one may also see the Woodworm dish, a fourteen foot long ceremonial food trough, carved many years ago in the form of a giant woodworm. It has a long segmented body, feet like a human being, and a human face with round, fat cheeks. And near Tukekan, in the totem park of Klukwan there is a totem pole showing the girl holding her woodworm pet in her arms.

* * *

The Killisnoo Beaver

The use of the Beaver as a crest of the *Decitan* clan of Tlingit Ravens is traced to an experience with a supernatural beaver. A chief of the Decitan who are principally from the vicinity of Angoon or Killisnoo once kept a small beaver which he had captured, as a pet. He was fascinated by its cunning ways and its clean habits and before long was giving it more attention than he accorded to members of his own household. On this account considerable jealousy arose, and some of the clansmen began abusing the pet beaver out of spite.

The beaver appealed to the Chief to end the ill-treatment it was receiving from everybody and demanded that his tormentors be punished. This the chief would not do so the beaver prepared to get revenge. Secretly it began composing songs in which it invoked the aid of certain spirits. Then it dived into its pond whereupon it changed into a giant beaver. In this form it secretly dug great tunnels beneath every house in the entire village. Nobody knew what the beaver was up to since it always resumed its natural form whenever it was among people. One day it went into the forest and fashioned a beautiful spear with its teeth. When it was finished it hid the spear in a hollow tree and went back to the village. But a passing hunter, noticing the fresh chips, investigated and found the weapon. Since it was so unusual he brought it into the village and showed it to the chief. Everybody came to see the remarkable weapon for it was the finest craftsmanship they had ever seen. The chief questioned each man, trying to find who had made it, but each denied making it or ever having seen such a spear.

Finally the beaver came forward saying, "That is my make!" The statement coming from a little beaver sounded so ridiculous that everybody including the chief laughed.

The beaver was enraged at their derision. "You were lying when you said you made that spear," said the chief. At that, the beaver grasped the weapon away from him, saying, "I will show you that I am strong enough to use it," whereupon it thrust the chief through the heart. Then it slapped its tail against the earth with tremendous force.

The village shook as if in a terrific earthquake, then fell apart and disappeared into the beaver's excavations. Not a house in the village was saved.

Those who escaped with their lives, knowing the cause of the disaster, took the beaver as their crest. They made a Beaver Hat and since then, people who can trace their ancestry to the Decitan clan may have the Beaver insignia on their blankets and carve it on their totem poles. It may always be recognized by its two prominent teeth, its cross-hatched tail and by the magic spear which it sometimes holds.

* * *

Yax-te Totem Pole at Auke Village Site

A lone totem pole stands beside Glacier Highway, 16 miles north of Juneau to mark the site of an old Auke village once known as Auke-an (Little Lake Village), and the principal town of the Auke *Kwan* or "group" of Tlingit Indians.

When gold was discovered near the present city of Juneau, the Aukes abandoned all of their own villages and moved to Juneau where they built their new homes along the beach now threaded by Willoughby Avenue. Before long not a house was left at any of the old locations.

The pole was erected in 1941 by the Indian Division of the Civilian Conservation Corps under direct supervision of Mr. Linn Forrest of the U.S. Forest Service to whom I am indebted for the facts concerning the project and the legends related on the pole. The actual carving was done by three Indians: St. Clair of Hoonah and two local Auke assistants.

In the remote past, remembered only in legend, the Aukes were warring with another band of Indians that dwelt in the vicinity of Klawock. A war party of the Aukes sought to surprise the enemy on one of their raids, but somehow news of the approaching fleet of war canoes preceded it, and the intended victims had already escaped into the forest when the party arrived. That is, all excepting one old woman, too weak and crippled to accompany the fleeing band.

Expecting to be killed by the enemy, the old woman had taken a red paint stone and had drawn a design on her chin, forehead and both cheeks. She was found alone by the first three warriors to land who happened to be the nephews of the great Auke chief, *Yees-ka-nachl* (One who gets rich all at once).

The nephews whose names were *Yick-du-seen*, *Dah-klen*, and *Yun-de-ahch*, were very curious about the meaning of the designs which covered the old woman's face and asked her the meaning of them. Refusing to tell them, she said it was a secret

which would die with her. Threats of starvation and torture were of no avail; nothing they did could make her talk. But after a while, the old woman became convinced that they meant her no harm, so she told them she would let them share her secret. First, she went down to the beach and washed off the markings with salt water. When she returned she told them that the design represented her clan symbol or tribal crest which was *Yax-te,* the constellation in the sky known to us as *Ursa Major* and the *Big Dipper*. Because they had spared her, the old woman conferred the symbol on the chief, Yees-ka-nachl, who thereafter displayed it as his principal crest, as did his descendants to this day. It is a curious co-incidence that these Indians saw in the constellation, not a big dipper, as we do, but a big bear-like animal like the Romans who saw a big *she bear* (Ursa Major).

THE KILLISNOO BEAVER. (Saxman Totem Cluster), See story. U. S. Forest Service Photo.

Reading the pole from top to bottom, the first figure or the one that surmounts the pole is Raven, symbolizing Yees-ka-nachl's phratry. The design on his breast represents his heart which was supposed to be in his stomach.

The faces that appear on the shaft of the pole are first, Szk-e-ney or Magpie, one of Raven's associates in the quest for food. Its name means "arrow" because he flew straight as an arrow. Raven would order it to fly in search of food saying, "go up, go up" and then when he was directly over his quarry Raven would order it down to the kill, saying "go down, go down, and get!"

The next figure is *Ha-sha-kcqu* which looks something like an eagle but has a face like a man. Once during their travels, Raven and Ha-sha-kcqu came to a village where the people had stored their winter's food in cedar boxes. Raven ordered Ha-sha-kcqu to run into the village shouting that a great band of enemies were coming to destroy them. The panicked villagers rushed into the forest and Raven and his companian ate their fill.

The third face is that of Robin, called *Shushk* in some accounts and *Teesk* in others. It is there to recall one of Raven's most infamous capers wherein he inveigled a lot of small birds to help him barbecue a salmon, and then by trickery, kept them away while he ate the fish. Robin scorched his breast while trying to find some fish among the glowing coals of the barbecue fire.

Next is *Kla-skque* or Blue Jay. There are two stories to account for his topknot. According to one, he was one of the birds cheated out of his share of the barbecued salmon by Raven, after which he tied up his hair in mourning. By the other account, Raven took a fine spruce root and with it tied a raindrop in Blue Jay's hair. Blue Jay is important to the Tlingit because his chattering will warn of an approaching storm when it would be dangerous to go out in a canoe.

The next figure is that of a small bird called *Yey-ku-du-hits*. He cried when cheated out of his share of the salmon and like no other bird, when he cries, according to the Tlingit, "his tears come out."

The face just above the bear-like figure of Yax-te is the very first princess of the Auke Kwan. Once when a superior force of enemies from the south caused the villagers to flee, she alone remained to face them. Because they had been abandoned, she claimed all the houses in the town. The enemy, having no place to stay, departed and war was averted. For this, the princess was remembered ever after.

The Dragon fly design on Yak-te's body is decora-tive only, and merely symbolizes his back bone and ribs. It is also the design on the chief's chest which supports him and was a popular design on the chests traded up and down the coast by the Tsimshian.

* * *

The Abraham Lincoln Totem Pole

It must have been shortly after the Purchase that they carved it. Nobody today remembers and nobody recorded the event in writing then. Chances are that there wasn't a literate man present at its dedication; certainly not a white man. But it is an undeniable fact that some ninety years ago, a totem pole honoring Abraham Lincoln was carved and erected by a band of Indians on a tiny island in Southeastern Alaska.

Although the Lincoln totem pole had been photographed in a cluster of other totem poles as early as 1889, it was not until 1924 when Judge James Wickersham called the nation's attention to it in an article in Sunset Magazine that it was generally recognized for what it actually was. By then it was already too late to learn definitely how it came to be carved and erected.

But Indian legends are still told in Alaska and when equated with known history and the results of ethnological research, something close to truth usually emerges. What happened may have been something like this. At the time of the Purchase of Alaska in 1867, about a third of the native Indians of the coastal rain forests of the Alaskan Panhandle were in abject slavery to other Indians. The powerful Haida and some of the Tlingit raided the coast as far south as Puget Sound and brought back captives for their own servants or for trade to Haida, Tsimshian or Tlingit tribesmen. Many were born in slavery. Other Indians gambled away their freedom or lost it in petty intra-tribal clashes. To harbor an escaped slave was unpardonable. This was how the Ganaxadi Ravens had made their mistake. Because they had given sanctuary to escaped slaves they were considered outlaws and had been harried from place to place until, weakened and without hope, they had settled on tiny Village Island there to make their last stand against powerful and implacable foes.

About this time the Purchase took place and the U.S. Government set up a Customs Station near the southern border of Alaska on Tongass Island to try to intercept smugglers from Canada. This was not far from Village Island and Ebbetts, Chief of the harried group asked permission to settle his people on the island under the protecting guns of the Americans. This request was granted and the little band built their village in the sanctuary for which they were most grateful.

It may have been a co-incidence that the Revenue Cutter stationed there was the *Lincoln*. In any event, the Indians soon learned that because of an act of Abraham Lincoln there would be no more slavery in Alaska and that they were safe at last. It was quite normal, therefore, that Chief Ebbetts would want to show his gratitude in the only way that he could . . . by erecting a monument to the memory of the great man responsible for their delivery from their enemies.

Northwest Coast Indians ordinarily carve in a highly stylized manner. But in this rare instance there was no stylization in the Lincoln figure. Some-one must have provided the carver with a picture of Lincoln; probably a lithograph of the Brady photograph of Lincoln at Antietam, standing in a tall hat, with his right elbow bent. At the base of the monument Ebbetts had Thleda, the Tsimshian carver, depict the tribal emblem, a huge stylized Raven. Surmounting the 55 foot pole was the realistic figure of Lincoln standing, with frock coat, silk hat, arms akimbo—so real that any schoolchild would recognize it instantly.

Time passed and the village dwindled as the residents moved to the white men's towns that were springing up, offering employment and diversion. Tongass was all but forgotten. One by one the totem poles crumbled and fell or were purloined by tourists and carried away. Not until 1923 when President Harding visited Alaska was any notice taken of the Lincoln totem pole. But at that time, Judge James Wickersham sought to have Harding's itinerary altered to include a side trip to Tongass village. He had hoped that such a visit might result in the site being declared a National Monument since it contained perhaps the second sculpture ever made of Lincoln. Unfortunately, the itinerary could not be changed and President Harding never saw the Lincoln totem pole.

Finally in 1939, the pole was taken down and, being beyond repair, a replica was carved while all that remained in the Lincoln figure was presented to the Territorial Museum at Juneau. Unfortunately the Indians who carved the replica now standing at Saxman, near Ketchikan, stylized the figure of Lincoln to the point where it bears but little resemblance to the original or to Lincoln. But the preserved figure may still be seen in the State Museum at Juneau. The arms are gone and the hat lacks its brim. But the sad, benign countenance of the Great

THE LOON TREE. (Saxman Totem Park). Honored here is a loon whose loud call guided a lost band of Indians from a fog-darkened bay into the sunlight. Beneath it is another way the story of Kats and his grisly bear wife and cubs is told. (See story)

155

Emancipator is there, still reflecting his deathless determination that all men shall be forever free.

* * *

The Story of Kadjuk with the Broken Wing

Kadjuk may have amused himself tossing pebbles at the marmots for they were his natural food and he hunted them in the mountains which form the eastern boundary of Tlingit country. But one day when Kadjuk dived at a marmot sitting on a mountain top, the little animal dashed for its den and Kadjuk, unable to check his flight, crashed on the rocks and broke his wing. Unable to rise and fly away, Kadjuk could think of no way to save his life. So to prepare for death which seemed inevitable, Kadjuk composed a death song and as the sun fell, started to sing.

A group of Yakutat Indians hunting goats on the mountainside, hearing the beautiful singing, began climbing upward, seeking its source. All night long they climbed, for the mountain was high. Reaching the top just as dawn broke, they saw the huge bird lying helpless in the rocks. They could have killed it easily but because of its beautiful song, had compassion. The broken wing was splinted and bound so well that it healed rapidly and Kadjuk could soon fly again. Grateful for the Indians' help, Kadjuk told them who he was and promised them that he would forever after be the guardian spirit of that particular band.

So when the hunters returned to Yakutat they built a new community house and in honor of their new guardian, named it *Kadjut-Hit*. As the years passed and the clan grew in numbers it became necessary to build a new house to accommodate the overflow. This house was named *Drum House* but the heraldic screen on the rear wall told the story of *Kadjuk with the Broken Wing*. It may now be seen in the State Museum in Juneau.

* * *

Kats, the Famous Bear Hunter

Kats was a character out of Tlingit mythology known from one end of their country to the other and claimed as an ancestor by groups and individuals from Yakutat to Ketchikan. His unusual experience was the inspiration of totem poles and heraldic screens in several villages, some of which have been preserved in the State Museum or restored in the Totem Park at Saxman.

Kats hunted grisly bears for a living and was brave enough to seek them out in their dens where they hibernated, dispatching them with a short spear. On one occasion his dogs led him to a den which was occupied by a pair of grislys and he prepared to fight them as he always had in the past. But this time the male bear was too fast for him. With one swift slap it tossed Kats into the den then took off in pursuit of the dogs.

When Kats landed inside the cave, he accidentally came into contact with the she-grisly who fell in love with him. When the male bear returned to the den she threw him out and settled down to housekeeping with her new human mate.

Tlingit mythology tells us that all animals are really people in disguise and only take the form of animals when they are away from home. In the case of grisly bears, they wear their hides like overcoats. So to Kats the cave looked like a house and the female bear who had captured him appeared to be a woman.

Years went by like hours and before long Kats and his grisly bear wife had three children. Kats hunted hair seals for his bear family and for a time they lived together happily. But as the days went by Kats began to worry about the human family he had back in his native village. Finally he told his bear wife that he would like to return to his old home just to see if his family was all right. For a long time she refused but she eventually gave in to his pleading after he promised that he would not talk to his other wife or do anything for her family.

But when Kats got to his old home and saw the condition of his children he was saddened and ashamed for having neglected them. With nobody to hunt for them they were poor and nearly starved. So, breaking his promise to the she-grisly, he went hunting for them.

Not trusting her human mate, the bear had sent her cubs to spy on their father. When they saw him out hunting for his human kin they fell upon him as instructed, and tore him to pieces.

To this day, many Tlingit Indians claim descent from this unusual union. And because they are of half-grisly ancestry, none of them will eat grisly bear meat.

* * *

BIBLIOGRAPHY OF WORKS CONSULTED

ALASKAN, THE (1885-1905)—*A Sitka Newspaper*   State Historical Library, Juneau
BANCROFT, HUBERT H.—*History of Alaska*   San Francisco 1890
BANCROFT, HUBERT H.—*Native Races*   San Francisco 1883
BARBEAU, MARIUS—*Totem Poles of the Gitksan*   Ottawa 1929
BARBEAU, MARIUS—*Modern Growth of the Totem Pole*   Washington 1939
BARBEAU, MARIUS—*Totem Poles: By-Product of the Fur Trade, Scientific Monthly*
          Dec. 1942
BARBEAU, MARIUS—*Totem Poles, Vols. I & II*   Ottawa 1951
BARBEAU, MARIUS—*Haida Myths*   Ottawa 1953
BARBEAU, MARIUS—*Haida Carvers*   Ottawa 1957
BELCHER, CAPT. SIR EDWARD—*Narrative of a Voyage Round the World (1835-42)*
          London 1843
BOAS, FRANZ—*The Houses of the Kwakiutl, U.S. National Museum Proceedings*
          Washington, D.C. 1888
BOAS, FRANZ—*Social Organization and Secret Societies of the Kwakiutl Indians,*
     U.S. National Museum Report   Washington, D.C. 1895
BOAS, FRANZ—*Primitive Art*   Oslo 1927
CLEVELAND, R. J.—*Voyages, Maritime Adventures and Commercial Enterprises*
          London 1842
CULLISON, W. H.—*In the Wake of the War Canoe*   London 1915
COOK, CAPT. JAMES A.—*A Voyage to the Pacific Ocean 1776-1780*   London 1784
CORSER, H. P.—*Totem Lore*   Wrangell 1932
DAWSON, SIR GEORGE M.—*Queen Charlotte Islands*   Ottawa 1890
DEANS, JAMES—*Tales from the Totems of the Hidery*   Chicago 1899
DIXON, CAPTAIN GEORGE—*A Voyage Round the World 1758-88*   London 1789
DOCKSTADER, FREDERICK J.—*Indian Art in America*   Greenwich, Conn. 1961
DORSEY, GEORGE A.—*A Cruise among Haida and Tlingit Villages about Dixon's*
     Entrance. Appleton's Popular Science Monthly; June 1898
DOUGLAS, FREDERIC H. AND D'HARNONCOURT, RENE—*Indian Art of the U.S. Mu-*
     seum of Modern Art   New York 1941
EMMONS, GEORGE T.—*Basketry of the Tlingit. American Museum of Natural His-*
     tory   New York 1903
EMMONS, GEORGE T.—*The Chilkat Blanket. American Museum of Natural History*
          New York 1907
EMMONS, GEORGE T.—*The Whale House of the Chilkat. American Museum of*
     Natural History   New York 1916
MARCHAND, ETIENNE—*A Voyage Round the World 1790-92*   London 1801
MAURELLE, DON FRANCISCO ANTONIO—*Journal of a Voyage in 1775*   London 1781
MEARES, JOHN—*Meares Voyages*   London 1790
NIBLACK, ALBERT P.—*The Coast Indians of Southern Alaska and Northern British*
     Columbia; U.S. National Museum Report for 1888   Washington, D.C. 1890
PAALEN, WOLFGANG—*Totem Art—DYN 4-5*   Mexico, D.F. Dec. 1943
PORTLOCK, NATHANIEL—*Voyage Round the World 1785-88*   London 1789
RAVENHILL, ALICE—*The Natives of British Columbia*   Victoria 1938
ROQUEFEUIL, CAMILLE DE—*A Voyage Round the World 1816-19*   London 1823

SALISBURY, OLIVER M. *Quoth the Raven, a little Journey into the Primitive*
                                                              Seattle 1962
SHOTRIDGE, LOUIS—*House Posts and Screens and their Heraldy. The Museum
   Journal*   Philadelphia Sept. 1913
SIMPSON, SIR GEORGE—*Narrative of a Journey Round the World 1841-42* London 1847
SWANTON, JOHN R.—*The Haida of the Queen Charlotte Islands; Memoirs Amer.
   Museum of Natural History, Vol. 8, Pt. 1*   1905
SWANTON, JOHN R.—*Social Conditions, Beliefs and Linguistic Relations of the
   Tlingit Indians; 26th Annual Report; Bureau of American Ethnology*   1908
SWANTON, JOHN R.—*Haida Texts and Myths—Bulletin 29; Bureau of American
   Ethnology*   Washington, D.C. 1905
SWANTON, JOHN R.—*Tlingit Myths and Texts—Bulletin 39; Bureau of American
   Ethnology*   Washington, D.C. 1909
VANCOUVER, CAPT. GEORGE—*A Voyage of Discovery, 1790-95.*   London 1798
FROBESE, F. E.—*The Origin and Meaning of the Totem Poles* .. .. Sitka 1897
GARFIELD, VIOLA E.—*Tsimshian Clan and Society. U. of Wash.*   Seattle 1939
GARFIELD, VIOLA E., AND FORREST, LINN A.—*The Wolf and the Raven*   Seattle 1948
GODDARD, PLINY EARLE—*The Indians of the Northwest Coast*   New York 1934
GREEN, JONATHAN—*Journal of a Tour on the Northwest Coast of America in the
   Year 1829*   New York 1915
GUNTHER, ERNA—*Indians of the Northwest Coast—Taylor Museum and Seattle
   Art Museum Publication*   1951
HARRISON, CHARLES—*Ancient Warriors of the North Pacific*   London 1925
HOWAY, F. W.—*A Yankee Trader on the Northwest Coast 1791-1795; Wash. Hist.
   Quarterly Vol. XXI #2 April 1930*   Seattle 1930
INVERARITY, ROBT. BRUCE—*Art of the Northwest Coast*   Berkeley 1950
JEFFERYS, THOMAS—*Voyages from Asia to America*   London 1761
JENNESS, DIAMOND—*The Indians of Canada*   Ottawa 1932
JEWITT, JOHN R.—*Narrative of the Adventures and Sufferings of John R. Jewitt*
                                                              New York 1815
JONES, LIVINGSTON F.—*A Study of the Tlingits of Alaska*   New York 1914
KEITHAHN, E. L.—*On the Origin of the Totem Pole; Proceedings, Alaska Science
   Conference 1951.*   Mt. McKinley National Park.
KOTZEBUE, OTTO VON—*A Voyage of Discovery into the South Sea and Beering's
   Strait 1815-18*   London 1821
KRAUSE, AUREL—*Die Tlinkit Indianer*   Jena 1885
KRIEGER, HERBERT W.—*Some Aspects of Northwestern Coast Indian Art; The
   Scientific Monthly, Sept. 1926*
KRIEGER, HERBERT W.—*Archaeological and Ethnological Studies in Southeast
   Alaska; Smithsonian Misc. Collections Vol. 78 #7*   1926
LANGSDORFF, G. H. VON—*Voyages and Travels, 1803-07*   London 1814
LA PEROUSE, J. F. G. DE—*A Voyage Round the World 1785-88*   London 1798
LISIANSKY, UREY—*A Voyage Round the World 1803-06*   London 1814
MACKENZIE, ALEXANDER—*Mackenzie's Voyages*   London 1801
MALASPINA, DON ALEXANDRO—*Malaspina's Voyages 1789-94*   Madrid 1885